AF006

MASSIMILIANO AFIERO

AXIS FORCES
6

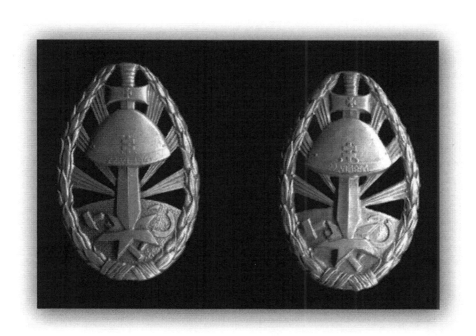

WW2 AXIS FORCES

The Axis Forces 006 - First edition April 2018 by Soldiershop.com.
Cover & Art Design by soldiershop factory. ISBN code: 978-88-93273435

In merito alla specifica serie Italia storia ebook serie Ritterkreuz l'editore Soldiershop informa che non essendone l'autore ne il primo editore del materiale pervenuto dall'associazione Ritterkreuz, declina ogni responsabilità in merito al suo contenuto di testi e/o immagini e la sua correttezza. A tal proposito segnaliamo che la pubblicazione Ritterkreuz tratta esclusivamente argomenti a carattere storico-militare e non intende esaltare alcun tipo di ideologia politica presente o del passato cosi come non intende esaltare alcun tipo di regime politico del secolo precedente ed alcuna forma di razzismo.

Note editoriali dell'edizione cartacea

The Axis Forces number 6 – April 2018

Direction and editing
Via San Giorgio, 11 – 80021 AFRAGOLA (NA) - ITALY
Managing and Chief Editor: Massimiliano Afiero
Email: maxafiero@libero.it - **Website**: www.maxafiero.it
Contributors

Stefano Canavassi, Carlos Caballero Jurado, Rene Chavez, Carlo Cucut, Daniel Fanni, Dmitry Frolov, Antonio Guerra, John B. Köser, Lars Larsen, Christophe Leguérandais, Giuseppe Lundari, Eduardo M. Gil Martínez, Peter Mooney, Ken Niewiarowicz, Erik Norling, Raphael Riccio, Marc Rikmenspoel, Charles Trang, Cesare Veronesi, Sergio Volpe

Editorial

Hi everybody, our magazine is getting more and more interesting, but we still need your collaboration to continue to rise and above all, to continue to improve our contents. In order to do this it is necessary that you send us your positive or negative comments, about our articles. Knowing what really matters to our readers is essential to bring forward and better guide our historical research. In each new issue we always try to tackle different and varied subjects, to try to please everyone. Some reports have already arrived and we are trying to widen the topics covered in our magazine to all the Axis nations and to all foreign voluntary units, trying to deal with unpublished topics and subjects that have not yet been adequately told by official historiography. In this new issue, we start with an article dedicated to Kampfgruppe Rehmann *on the Baltic front in the summer of 1944, we continue with a biography of Albert Frey, an officer in the* Leibstandarte Adolf Hitler *and a photographic reportage about the French volunteers on the Eastern front. You will find an excerpt of a new book by our friend and collaborator, Lars Larsen, dedicated to Danish volunteers in the* Waffen SS. *Then we report the second part of the work on the Hungarian armored units on the Eastern front, a wonderful article on the Folgore paratroopers division in Africa, another photographic reportage dedicated to the SS-Hauptsturmführer Hans-Jörg Hartmann (first part) and finally there will be an article on the decorations assigned to the Slovak soldiers who fought in Russia. Happy reading to everyone and see you in the next number.*

Massimiliano Afiero

Contents

Langemarck

in World War Two 1939-1945

The Kampfgruppe Rehmann, summer 1944
by Massimiliano Afiero

SS-Ostubaf. Conrad Schellong.

SS-Ostuf. Wilhelm Rehmann.

On 12 July 1944, the SS central command (*SS-Hauptamt*) contacted the *Sturmbrigade Langemarck* headquarters to issue new orders: *SS-Ostubaf.* Schellong was ordered to quickly organize a battalion for transfer to the front lines on the Eastern Front, as reinforcement for the *III.SS-Pz.Korps* under Felix Steiner. The SS corps, consisting among other units the *SS Nordland* Division and the *SS Nederland* Brigade, after having held out for months in the Narva bridgehead, was readying to pull back further to the west, on the Blue Mountains, along a new defensive line designated *Tannenbergstellung* that ran along the road that led from Narva to Riga. This was aimed at avoiding being trapped by the new Soviet offensive launched in the Baltic region by forces under General Govorov. Schellong decided to send *I.Bataillon* led by *SS-Hstuf.* Rehmann[1], reinforced with other brigade support elements.

Kampfgruppe Rehmann

Kdr: SS-Hauptsturmführer Rehmann
Adjutant: SS-Ustuf. van Leemputten
Artzt: Leutnant Dr. Hertgens
1.Kp.: *SS-Untersturmführer* Swinnen
2.Kp.: *SS-Untersturmführer* van Moll
3.Kp.: *SS-Untersturmführer* D'Haese
4.(s)Kp.: *SS-Untersturmführer* van Ossel

The *4.Kompanie* of the *Kampfgruppe* also had a *Pak Zug*, an anti-tank platoon, commanded by *SS-Ustuf.* Laperre. On 19 July 1944, Rehmann and his companies began the long trip towards the front at Narva. A few days later they arrived at Toila, in Estonia, where the headquarters of *III.SS-Pz.Korps* under *SS.-Gruf.* Steiner was located. Steiner personally inspected *I./Langemarck* , quickly deciding to make some changes to the unit's structure. Accordingly, the 4th Company of the *Kampfgruppe* had to parcel out its machine guns and mortars to the three infantry companies, while *SS-Ustuf.* Van Ossel and his staff were transferred to an Estonian SS company that had lost all of its officers in battle. This transfer of a Flemish officer to an Estonian unit fit into the *Waffen SS* concept that aimed at total integration of the various European populations. On 25 July 1944, the rest of the battalion, numbering about 450 men, under the command of *SS-Hstuf.* Wilhelm Rehmann, assumed positions on "Orphanage Hill" (*Kinderheim Höhe*) on *Tannenbergstellung*.

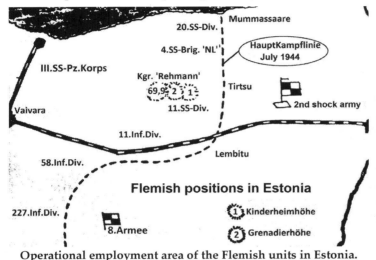

Operational employment area of the Flemish units in Estonia.

SS-Gruf. Felix Steiner

Disposition of Flemish units on the *Tannenbergstellung*.

The German defensive line along the *Tannenbergstellung* was anchored on the Blue Mountains (*Blauberg*, or in Estonian the heills of Sinimäed), which was a series of three hills called *Kinderheim* (Orphanage), *Grenadier* (Grenadier), and *69.9* (*Liebhöhe*, or Love Hill), which dominated all of the surrounding terrain as far as the coast. To the north of the *Langemarck* positions were the Dutch volunteers of the *SS Nederland* Division defending a line of bunkers that stretched as far as the Gulf of Finland. To the south was a *Kriegsmarine* infantry company and nearby there were other battalions consisting of Estonian, Latvian, Danish and Norwegian volunteers. The Flemish companies were dug in along a narrow stretch of ground, about six hundred meters long, between *Kinderheim* Hill and the edge of a forest from which the arrival of the Soviets was expected. The bunker with the *Kampfgruppe* staff was situated on the eastern side of the *Kinderheim*. The bunker with Dr. Hertgens' aid station was on the north-east side of Love Hill. *1.Kompanie* under *SS-Ustuf.* Swinnen was to the right (south) of *3.Kompanie* under *SS-Ustuf.* D'Haese was on the left (north), while *2.Kompanie* under *SS-Ustuf.* van Moll was in the center. Ther anti-tank guns were sited to support the companies. *SS-Hstuf.* Rehmann had the *Pak* under *SS-Uscha.* D'Hollander emplaced on the *Kinderheim*, a position that its gunners were not happy about. The *Pak* under Reeb was emplaced along the road that led from the forest, north of *Grenadier* Hill, and the *Pak* under *SS-Uscha.* Grootaers was to the right of that of *Uscha.* Reeb.

A *Pak 40* on the *Tannenbergstellung*, July 1944.

SS-Ustuf. van Leemputten.

SS-Ustuf. Georg D'Haese.

The Soviets attack

On 26 July, the Soviets unleashed a hurricane of fire against the positions defended by the European *Waffen SS* volunteers; the enemy artillery fire was particularly devastating against the Flemish positions on *Kinderheim* Hill, hitting the trenches and bunkers on the summit of the hill. Most of the runners and the medical personnel who were there were killed or wounded. Rehmann and his adjutant, *SS-Ustuf.* van Leemputten[2], were seriously wounded. During the night, the dead were buried and the wounded transferred to the *III.SS-Pz. Korps* field hospital. Battalion command was assumed by the *3.Kompanie* commander, *SS-Ustuf.* Georg D'Haese[3], who had also been slightly wounded. According to the testimony of some veterans, after having been cured of his throat wound and declared fir for duty, instead of returning directly to his men, Rehmann reported to *SS-Ogruf.* Steiner. The meeting between the two men was brief but stormy and the result was that Steiner decided to leave command of the Flemish *Kampfgruppe* in the hands of the young

D'Haese. Once the storm of artillery fire had ended, a column of Soviet tanks backed by infantry attacked the hill; German artillery quickly took them under fire, stopping the first wave, but Soviet artillery then joined in, allowing the tanks to resume the attack. Several positions defended by SS grenadiers of *Danmark* were overcome, as were the outposts of *2.* and *3.Kp* of *Langemarck*, on the eastern crest of *Kinderheim*, which had to be abandoned.

A 75mm *Pak 40* in firing position.

SS grenadiers on the Tannenberg line.

SS defensive position with an *MG-34* under attack.

Soon after, most of the eastern side of the hill fell into Soviet hands. A series of desperate counterattacks were launched and bloody hand-to-hand fighting ensued on the hilltop; using entrenching tools and bayonets in close quarters against the enemy, the Flemings were able to push back the Soviets. On the battalion's northern flank the *Kampfgruppe's* anti-tank guns were in position. One after another, the guns belonging to Grootaers, D'Hollander and Reeb came under enemy fire. The commander of the *Pak Zug, SS-Ustuf.* Marcel Laperre[4] , also was wounded. *SS-Uscha.* D'Hollander, realizing that his position was about to fall into enemy hands, directed his men to leave their position and then damaged his gun so that it could not be used by the Soviets. He was killed due to improper handling of the explosive charge while he was spiking the gun. The *Pak* belonging to *SS-Uscha.* Reeb was damaged the next day, 27 July, following the explosion of a shell nearby. The gun crew was unscathed, but the gun itself had to be brought to the rear to be repaired. Soon thereafter the gunners were assigned to the infantry companies and fought as simple infantrymen for the rest of the campaign.

Sturmmann Dries Anseeuw.

Testimony of Flemish *Sturmmann* Dries Anseeuw who served in the anti-tank squad of *SS-Uscha.* Eduard Reeb, during this first day of combat[5]:
"...As soon as day broke, we had completed our preparations. But a Dutch officer arrived who ordered us to abandon our positions. We had sited our gun near a house and to the left of the road. The left side of the road was however occupied by another unit and thus we had to find another position on the right side of the road. The terrain in the area was level. In front of us was Orphanage Hill, on the right was Grenadier Hill, and behind us was Love Hill. We had to move our gun before full daylight broke...the new position was excellent. The gun was protected by three tree trunks laid together. The gun could traverse easily to the right or to the left. There was a trench near the position and a foxhole further away. There were also other sheltered spots for our ammunition. In the meantime it had become

daylight and we took shelter in our holes. I had time to look around me and near Grenadier Hill I saw another Pak *in position, but I did not know which gun it was* (probably that of Jef Grootaers, author's note). *The sector remained quiet, but not for long...*

A *Pak 40* opening fire against Soviet tanks, Summer 1944.

Some heavy bombers flew over our position. The earth shook and several bombs were dropped. We stayed under cover in our holes...The three hills were hit heavily. The air attack lasted for about an hour, and then it became quiet again. Thank God, our position was spared. We had survived our first baptism of fire and had only to await the next attack. The Geschützführer *and the* Richtschütze *were walking around the gun when the new attack began. Stalin Organs, light and heavy artillery, mortars, and whatever else could fire hit our positions. Orphanage Hill and Grenadier Hill were hit again; rocks, earth and trees flew all around the heights. Then the fire also began to hit positions further back, the flat area and Love Hill. Shells, splinters, fragments, rocks all began to rain down on our heads. Something fell into my hole with a loud thud. It had fallen along my right side, near my pistol holster, and had hit the heel of my right boot.*

An anti-tank position with an *MG-34.*

SS grenadier in a foxhole.

A *Pak 40* damaged by Soviet fire and abandoned.

I was shocked and expected something to explode suddenly, but that did not happen! I was paralyzed and in no condition to leave my hole. After a little time had passed I began to search for what had actually happened in my hole. It was a fragment about twenty centimeters long and five wide. My belt had been cut in two and my holster had been damaged. The heel of my boot had been only crushed. You have to have luck as a soldier. But it wasn't over, the enemy fire continued and shell splinters continued to fall...I couldn't see anything around me except for dust and smoke. The three trees near our position had disappeared, and in their place only burnt trunks remained. The shelling continued for a long time. We began to call each other to determine that we had suffered no losses. The soldier's luck had not forsaken us. We were scared, but we had all held fast. We didn't know how much time had passed, but surely by now it was afternoon. As soon as the fire decreased its intensity we heard the rumble of engines and all of us, as though we had just received an order, poked our heads from our holes. The noise came from three German tanks that had stopped to the right of our gun and then moved about twenty meters from our position. This seemed to be a good thing for us! We scanned the terrain in the direction of the road that led from the left of Orphanage Hill, but there was nothing suspicious to be seen.

Attack by Soviet tanks and infantry, Summer 1944.

A *Waffen-SS* soldier.

SS grenadiers ready to attack.

A *T-34* viewed by a German observer.

Suddenly we heard the men of the Panzers exchange orders and soon after they began to fire. We kept watching, but could see nothing. We heard more orders come from the tanks, after which they began to pull back. Only the third tank, near our Pak, *made a wide turn, exposing its rear to the enemy. It was able to travel only three meters! A crack and its turret flew into the air. Red and black flames leapt into the air. It had been a direct hit. I saw two men run towards Love Hill, and then we heard shouts. We stayed in our holes, when suddenly the alarm was given; A T-34 was approaching at full speed along the road in our direction. Now we were in battle! Everything happened quickly. We called the Geschützführer and the Richtschütze; I was already by the gun but neither saw nor heard the two men. As we later discovered, the two men, sheltering in another trench, were dazed by the explosion of a shell near their position. In view of the fact that neither of them showed up, I took the place of the* Richtschütze *and adjusted the gun's sights for three hundred meters and asked for a* Panzergranate *(an armor-piercing round). The round was loaded into the gun and everything happened quickly; because a lot of time had already been lost looking for the other gunners. I took aim, I had the T-34 square in my sights, and then I fired. Hit! A direct hit! It was the same tank that shortly before had knocked out the German tank. An enormous flame developed, the turret was knocked off sideway and red and black flames began to issue from the hulk of the tank. We wanted to look for the other gunners but there was no time because a second T-34 was approaching.*

A *Waffen-SS* anti-tank crew manning a *Pak 40*.

SS grenadier in battle.

SS grenadiers under Soviet artillery fire.

I set the sight for four hundred meters and loaded another armor-piercing round. Exactly as had happened with the first T-34, this one was also hit. Two rounds in a few minutes, and it became quiet once again. We scanned the road again. A third T-34 that was following the other two also approached…

Our gun was already loaded. I set the sights for seven hundred meters. Tension rose when I began to get the tank in my sight picture. I pushed the button and like the other two, the tank caught fire. The third T-34 burned like a torch on the road between the little house and Orphanage Hill. After having destroyed three tanks, we stayed calm and returned to our holes with our eyes fixed on the open terrain to the left of Orphanage Hill".

SS-Uscha. **Schrijnen with the Knight's Cross.**

A *Pak 40* with a crew of Flemish volunteers.

Hulk of Soviet *T-34* tank destroyed.

The Knight's Cross for Sturmmann Remi Schrijnen

The only gun that was still able to fire was that of Grootaers, served by *SS-Sturmmann* Remi Schrijnen, who was left by himself after all of the other gun crew were either wounded or killed. The gun's shield had been partly destroyed and the extractor was also damaged. D'Haese had ordered him not to let himself be seen and to open fire only at the last instant. From his position the Flemish corporal saw the enemy tanks passing alongside at a close distance; it was an opportunity not to be lost. Before being completely reached by the enemy tank column, he decided to act. Schrijnen loaded the gun and fired, loaded again and fired again, continuing to fire until his ammunition ran out, but not before knocking out three *Josef Stalin* tanks, four *T-34s*, and having damaged at least another pair. Having finally been discovered by the Soviet tankers, the Fleming's position was hit numerous times. A large *Stalin* tank managed to get dangerously close to Schrijnen's gun, but at the last moment was hit by a direct hit. In the explosion that followed, Schrijnen himself was wounded, but the line had been held. The other enemy tanks withdrew. Fallen next to his gun, after having lost consciousness, Schrijnen miraculously escaped being crushed by the tracks of the enemy tank; once the battle was over he regained consciousness and aside from suffering a few splinters in his body and a state of confusion due to the strong explosion, he could consider himself safe. The following day, still in a confused state, he was given aid by tankers from *Nordland*. For his exemplary performance, Schrijnen's action was mentioned in the *Wehrmacht* Bulletin of 5 August 1944. Two days earlier he had been decorated with the Iron Cross First Class and with the Wound Badge in gold. On 13 August 1944, *SS-Ogruf.* Steiner recommended Schrijnen for the *Ehrensblattspange des Deutschen Heeres*[6].

SS-Uscha. **Remi Schrijnen.**

Award ceremony for the *Ritterkreuz*.

On 28 August, the recommendation was upgraded, thanks to the intercession of Schellong, for the award of the Knight's Cross with this justification: "...*On 26 July 1944, at 09:00, the Soviets attacked with three T-34 tanks along the Narwa-Reval highway. Schrijnen destroyed two T-34's at a distance of about four hundred meters. At 15:00 in the afternoon the Soviets attacked again with infantry forces, supported by artillery and heavy mortar fire. Schrijnen destroyed another two T-34 tanks and a* Stalin. *Another T-34 was also damaged. Its crew managed to escape from the vehicle. The damaged tank was probably towed away during the night. On 27 July 1944, at 04:00, Schrijnen's gun was shifted about four hundred meters north of* Kinderheim *Hill, to the left of the Narwa-Reval highway. Schrijnen spotted a concentration of eleven enemy tanks that were preparing to attack. The Soviet tanks approached the highway from the north. At a distance of seven hundred meters, Schrijnen hit and destroyed a T-34. The other T-34s began to take the anti-tank gun under fire. Schrijnen soon destroyed a* KV II. *Immediately afterwards, however, the anti-tank gun sustained a direct hit...*".

Many years after the end of the war, Schrijnen wanted to correct part of the citation, specifying that he had never destroyed a *KV II* tank during the battle, but only *T-34* and *Josef Stalin* tanks. The award of the *Ritterkreuz* was not made official until 21 September 1944, along with his promotion to *Unterscharführer* (skipping the rank of *Rottenführer*). In early October of the same year an official ceremony was held at the Selschau-Beneschau training camp near Prague. In his role as commander, Konrad Schelling personally awarded the Knight's Cross to Schrijnen.

Flemish grenadiers, Summer 1944.

The Flemish volunteers in battle

On the same day of 26 July many other *Langemarck* officers were wounded or killed in combat; the commander of *1.Kompanie, Ustuf.* Albert Swinnen, was wounded and was replaced by *Ustuf.* Josef van Bockel, who was killed in the fighting the next day. The commander of *2.Kompanie, SS-Ustuf.* Henri van Moll, was also killed in combat. Among the few officers who survived was Doctor Hertgens, who was busy saving human lives at his aid station. During the night between 26 and 27 July the positions defended by the naval infantry on the southern flank of *Langemarck* were overrun by a new enemy armor attack, threatening the bunkers held by the Flemings and by the *Norge*. One anti-tank squad, led by *Uscha.* Illum, pushed as far ahead as no-man's land, managing to destroy numerous enemy tanks at close range. At dawn on 27 July, Soviet artillery began again to hit the Flemish defensive positions, before unleashing a new tank and infantry attack; fighting alongside a German disciplinary battalion, the Flemings tried desperately to defend the *Kinderheim Höhe*. Under heavy enemy pressure, *Ustuf.* D'Haese had his men pull back from the eastern crest of Grenadier Hill, more to the west.

A defensive position on the *Kinderheim hill*, Summer 1944.

A Flemish *SS-Rottenführer*.

Around 21:30 a Flemish assault group reinforced with Latvian and Estonian elements, attacked the Soviet positions of the eastern crest of the *Kinderheim*. There was hand-to-hand fighting in the darkness during which the enemy forward positions were taken one after the other. With the support of artillery, the Soviet machine guns on the *Kinderheim* were silenced. With only limited forces available, the SS assault group was not able to remain to defend the positions on the hill, and therefore withdrew. In a bunker on *Grenadier Hill*, the *Kampfgruppe Langemarck* staff, which had been reduced to only three men, these being *Ustuf*. Georg D'Haese, his adjutant and *SS-Ustuf*. Groenvynck, began to prepare orders for the following day.

SS Grenadiers moving to attack with a *MG-42*.

A mortar manned by SS soldiers.

SS-Ustuf. Siegfried Scheibe.

Blood on Grenadier Hill

At the end of the day, the Flemings were entrenched on *Grenadier Hill*. Many men had been killed or wounded. Unfortunately about fifty soldiers of the *Kampfgruppe* had remained on *Orphanage Hill*. On 28 July, the Soviets returned to attack in force, always preceded by a massive barrage by their artillery. The focal point of the battle was the same as it had been the day before, *Orphanage Hill*, where Estonian and Soviet soldiers were locked in bitter close-quarter fighting. During those hours, *III.SS-Pz.Korps* decided to launch a final assault in an attempt to retake the *Kinderheim*. The following units were designated for the attack: *5.* and *6./Norge, Kampfgruppe Langemarck,* and the remnants of *SS-Frw.Rgt. 47(estnisches Nr. 3)*, all under command of *SS-Stubaf.* Scheibe, commander of *II./Norge.*

After a brief artillery preparatory fire, the assault force attacked the western crest of *Kinderheim* Hill with Flemish volunteers led by *SS-Ustuf*. Leemputten. The SS grenadiers ended up in the enemy trenches and engaging in furious close-quarter fighting. The Soviets sent in reinforcements and beat back the enemy attack. After *SS-Stubaf*. Scheibe was wounded, the units withdrew to *Grenadier Hill*. *SS-Ustuf*. D'Haese and many other

Flemish officers were wounded during the fighting. The positions of the SS volunteers on the eastern side of the hill were overrun, but the Soviets were stopped at the last moment on the summit of the hill. From that moment, all attempts to retake *Kinderheim* were abandoned. *SS-Ustuf.* Walter van Leemputten was seriously wounded and was brought to the aid station in a disastrous condition. He died on 17 August 1944 at the *III.SS-Pz.Korps* field hospital. Also on 29 June, the fourth day of the battle along the *Tannenbergstellung*, Soviet artillery continued to heavily shell the German positions, in particular *Grenadier Hill* and the village of Chundinurk. *Grenadier hill* was transformed into a huge mushroom cloud of smoke and dust. Then the Soviets attacked with numerous infantry formations supported by a heavy concentration of tanks. German artillery quickly joined in the action but was able to accomplish little against the formidable mass of armor; the forward positions were overrun almost immediately, while other positions were simply bypassed.

Estonian volunteers on the *Tannenbergstellung*, 1944.

Soviet tank and infantry.

A Flemish machine gun crew in combat.

The toughest fighting naturally took place on *Grenadier Hill*; the survivors of *II./Norge*, of the Flemish *Kampfgruppe*, the Estonians of the 20th SS Division, and what remained of a *Kriegsmarine* battalion continued to fight on as small groups, counting on themselves alone and with no support from other forces. There were explosions and fires everywhere. From the eastern side of *Orphanage Hill*, the Soviets fired their heavy weapons, pummeling everything and everyone, including their own troops. Some *Nordland Panzers* and *StuG*, led by *SS-Ostubaf.* Paul-Albert Kausch, commander of

Pz.Abt.11, were able to launch a desperate armored attack and to drive off the Soviets once again. On 30 July 1944, the sacrifice of *Kampfgruppe Langemarck* was over: of the about five hundred men who were present on 25 July, only about fifty were still fit for combat.

A wounded *Waffen-SS* soldier on the Tannenberg line.

SS grenadier in battle.

Soviet infantry and tanks on the attack.

A *Waffen-SS* sniper engaging the enemy.

Deployed along a sector of the front about two miles wide, the Flemings found themselves still facing numerous enemy attacks. At the end, the Soviets were not able to break the defensive line held by the European volunteers, suffering so many casualties that they decided to suspend any further offensive operations in the *Tannenbergstellung* sector. Despite the huge commitment of forces, the Soviets had been stopped cold by the fierce resistance of the Germanic *Waffen SS* volunteers. Feeling that they were beaten, the Soviets also abandoned the heavily contested positions on *Orphanage Hill*, but not before having killed all of the captured wounded prisoners who could not walk. During the course of the first week of August, *SS-Usftuf.* D'Haese was called to *III.SS-Pz.Korps* headquarters whose commander, Steiner, personally congratulated the Flemish officer, praising the valor of his soldiers. D'Haese was subsequently awarded the Iron Cross First

Class. When he returned to his men, he learned that they had been withdrawn to the rear for a period of rest. On 12 August, a Soviet battalion passed through the German lines, pushing as far as the *III.SS-Pz.Korps* headquarters at Toila; the Flemings were once again called to action. For a full day they were engaged in hard fighting to push back the Soviets. A few days later, most of the lightly wounded returned, raising the strength of the unit to about a hundred men. For a few days, the Flemings remained in reserve at Toila, after which they were transferred to the coast of northern Estonia, on the Gulf of Finland, to defend against any enemy landings. To this end, the battalion was issued new heavy weapons and a few artillery pieces. On 8 September 1944, *Kampfgruppe Langemarck* returned to the *Tannenbergstellung*, taking up positions in front of the *Kinderheim Höhe*. A group of naval infantry dressed in SS Uniforms were assigned as reinforcements. Only a few days later the withdrawal of German forces from Estonia began. In the meantime Belgium had been liberated by the Allies and as a consequence the flow of Flemish volunteers from the homeland ended abruptly.

Notes

[1] Wilhelm Rehmann, born 15 March 1912 in Hamburg, SS Number 174 532. After having served for a number of years in the Allgemeine-SS, at the beginning of the war Rehmann served in the army with *5./Inf.Rgt.461*. Having distinguished himself during the Polish campaign, he was awarded the Iron Cross Second Class. On 20 April 1941, Rehmann was promoted to *Obersturmführer der Waffen SS* and transferred to the *SS-Ergänzungs-Stelle 'Rhein'*, a recruiting center in Flanders. In April 1943, he was transferred to *10.SS-Pz.Div. 'Frundsberg'* where he served as *Zugführer* and *Kompanieführer* in a *Panzer-Grenadier Regiment*. During this period with the *Frundsberg*, he attended a company commander's course between July and August 1943. On 14 November 1943, he was assigned to *SS-Feldersatz-Bataillon 10* as a company commander.

[2] Walter van Leemputten, born 4 December 1914 in Putney, England.

[3] Georg D'Haese, born 4 August 1922 in Lede, in Flanders. Son of a Flemish nationalist, he enlisted in the *Waffen SS* on 23 May 1941 at the age of eighteen. D'Haese was assigned to *8.Kompanie* of the *Freiwilligen-Standarte 'Nordwest'*. When formation of the *Flemish Legion* began, D'Haese was transferred to its *3.Kompanie*. After training at Debica, he was promoted to *SS-Sturmmann*. Soon thereafter he was selected for training as a *Sturmpionier*, or assault engineer, and was sent to the engineer school in Dresden. While serving with *Flandern*, he was wounded twice and was awarded the Black Wound Badge and the Iron Cross Second Class. In September 1943, he was sent to an officer's course at the *SS-Junkerschule* at Bad Tölz, which he completed in March 1944. On 21 June 1944, he was promoted to *SS-Untersturmführer*.

[4] Marcel Laperre, born on 29 May 1923 in Bissegem, Flanders. A member of *Verdinaso*, after having joined the Flemish SS, in July 1943 he enlisted in the *Waffen SS*. After basic training he was invited to attend an officer's course at the *SS-Junkerschule* at Bad Tölz, which he completed in March 1944. On 21 June 1944, he was promoted to *SS-Untersturmführer*.

[5] Report by Drieu Anseeuw, dated 10 November 1997. From the book "*The Last Knight of Flanders*", pages 127, 129, 134 and 135. Born on 17 August 1925, Anseeuw was 18 years old when he fought on the Blue Mountains. Having survived that battle, he was awarded the Knight's Cross Second Class. Anseeuw continued to serve in *Langemarck* anti-tank units until the end of the war.

[6] This decoration began as a special honorific mention for all soldiers who had distinguished themselves in a combat action; the name, rank, and unit of the soldier were reported on a special list called the *Ehrenblatt des Deutschen Heeres*, published beginning on 22 July 1941. Beginning on 31 January 1944, Hitler decided to institute a "metal" version (*Ehrenblatt-Spange*), of the citation in the list of honor, to be assigned to all members of the German Army and of the *Waffen SS*. The metal badge was attached to the ribbon of the Iron Cross Second Class.

Bibliography
M. Afiero, "*The 27th Waffen SS Vol.Gren.Div. Langemarck'*", Schiffer Publishing
A. Brandt, "*The Last Knight of Flanders*", Schiffer Publishing Ltd.

Albert Frey
Knight's Cross with Oakleaves Holder of the Leibstandarte
by Peter Mooney

SS-Stubaf. **Frey with** *Ritterkreuz.*

Albert Frey was born on the 16th of February 1913, in Heidelberg. Just after his 20th birthday, he entered service with the *SS,* in mid-June 1933. He was placed with, what later became, *SS-Regiment Deutschland.* He remained with that formation until March 1937. He had progressed through the junior ranks in those years and by the end of 1936, he held the rank of *SS-Scharführer.* He was then sent to the SS Officers school at Braunschweig from March 1937, staying there for a year. He left there with the rank of *SS-Standartenoberjunker.* That was quickly followed on the 12th of March 1938, with promotion to *SS-Untersturmführer* and a move to the *Leibstandarte,* his 'home' for the remainder of his military career. On the 20th of April 1939, he received a further promotion to *SS-Obersturmfuhrer;* the rank he entered the Second World War with. Pre-war, Frey held the SA Sports Badge in Bronze, the Reichs Sports Badge in Bronze, the Austrian Annexation campaign medal and also the Sudetenland Annexation medal, with Prague Bar. He fought in Poland, earning the Second Class Iron Cross on the 25th of September 1939. He also moved west in 1940 and was awarded the First Class Iron Cross on the 30th of June, followed by the Infantry Assault Badge on the 3rd of October the same year. He had been given command of the *LAH's, 11.Kompanie* back at the start of August and this was followed by a promotion to *SS-Hauptsturmfuhrer* on the 9th of November 1940. His next campaign was in the Balkans in early 1941 and then he moved into Russia in mid-1941.

Two photos of Albert Frey whilst commanding the *11.Kompanie* **in Russia.**

Summer 1941, area of Nikolajew: from the left, Max Hansen, Wilhelm Weidenhaupt, Albert Frey and Joachim Peiper.

On the 16th of October that year he was given command of the *LAH's III Battalion*. The award of the German Cross in Gold came just over one month later, on the 17th of November 1941. Back on the 25th of October 1941, his commander, Sepp Dietrich, had recommended Frey for the award of the Knight's Cross of the Iron Cross, for the bridgehead his unit had established over the Mius River, north of Taganrog. It highlights his courage and cold-blooded determination and attributes the fast advance and capture of Taganrog to Frey's actions at the Mius River. This recommendation was not approved at that time. It could be these actions that resulted in the award the German Cross in Gold, as no recommendation for that medal is contained within his file? Towards the end of their first stint in Russia, on the 20th of April 1942, Frey was promoted to *SS-Sturmbannführer*. Ten days later he assumed command of the *I Battalion* within the *LAH*.

Albert Frey and his wife, prior to his return to Russia in 1943.

He moved with his men to France in the second half of 1942 and whilst there received further awards. The Royal Bulgarian Bravery Medal IV Class, 1st Grade came on the 6th of July, the Royal Romanian Medal with Swords followed on the 3rd of September, as well as the Russian Front Medal. It was then time to return to Russia. That return to Russia brought the *Leibstandarte* to the Kharkov area. They undertook a see-saw battle around this location during February and March 1943. Frey would witness significant losses within his Battalion, but also see some of his men recognised for their bravery during this very difficult fighting. He himself would also be recognised for his leadership of that Battalion during this time. One of his soldiers, *SS-Oberscharführer* Hermann Dahlke, took leadership of the remnants of Frey's *3.Kompanie* on the 14th of February, following the death of the 3 officers. This was also despite a recently arrived officer candidate, *SS-Standartenoberjunker* Gunther Zaag, being there too.

The *Stug* that supported the *3.Kompanie* at Bereka.

Bereka village on the horizon, the scene of the *3.Kompanie* battle.

German grenadiers and *Panzer* on the Kharkov front.

Zaag had not long returned from SS officers school, but Dahlke was a front line soldier, who seized the moment and led the remaining men to local victory at Bereka, ably assisted by one of the *LAH Sturmgeschütze*. Both Frey and Dahlke were proposed for the award of the Knight's Cross on the 2nd of March 1943. Frey's recommendation was short and to the point, reading as follows: *"Recommendation for the award of the Knight's Cross for SS-Sturmbannführer Albert Frey* [the document then lists existing awards and personal details], *I propose that the Commander of the* I./1.Panzer-Grenadier-Regiment/ LSSAH, SS-Sturmbannführer *Albert Frey, under the again adjoining duplicate of the Knight's Cross recommendation from the 25.10.1941 because in it and the recent heavy fighting and attacks, displayed personal courage and outstanding leadership of his Battalion and their higher preservation. (signed) Dietrich,* SS-Obergruppenführer und General der Waffen-SS. *(approved) Schmundt"*.

This second recommendation was approved the following day, the 3rd of March 1943; the same day that Dahlke also received his approval for the award of the Knight's Cross. The fighting at Bereka was witnessed by *SS-Sturmmann* Gerhard Dilling, then one of the surviving soldiers within the *3.Kompanie* at Bereka. Exactly sixty years after this action, February 2003, Dilling wrote a letter to his former commander, Albert Frey. The former radio operator's recollections went as follows: *"On the 14th of February 1943, we became aware of the fact that radio contact with the* 3.Kompanie *and* 1.Kompanie *had been lost. After repeating this situation to you (Frey) twice, you gave me the order to establish radio contact once again.*

Gerhard Dilling shown whilst at Bad Tölz in 1944, he was the writer of the letter to Frey and one of the witnesses to the Bereka fighting.

SS-Ustuf. Hermann Dahlke.

The 9.Kompanie of Der Führer *were moving up on the right hand side, so they were ordered to assist in the attack and the time of the attack was set for 11:00am. You gave me an accurate description of the way to Bereka. Move along the track towards the small forest, then turn 90 degrees to the left of this forest and continue for 2-3 Km, where I would find Bereka. As I advanced along this route, there was one* Stug *from Wiesemann's unit. I advanced through very deep snow and the temperature was freezing. I did take two photos of this area at that time and carried on. Despite the cold, I was sweating and had to use some snow to help cool me down. After I passed the forest, there was the sound of gunfire and on the right, I seen the village of Bereka. I had to cross two Balkas to reach the village and after crossing the first I noticed a small group of enemy soldiers moving towards my position. They were initially 100 metres away, so I ensured my rifle was fully loaded. When they came to within 30 metres I shouted to them to put up their hands. They did not do what I asked and as they came closer, I could see that the wind and snow was forcing them to keep their eyes closed. Thankfully, SS-Rottenführer Fuhring was moving behind them with his machine-pistol, so the situation came out well for us. I then moved into the village and came across SS-Oberscharführer Dahlke. My arrival had come too late, as they had already attacked in the early morning. This attack had produced enormous loss for the 3.Kompanie, with SS-Obersturmführer Gessner, SS-Untersturmführer Flocke and many of the NCOs being killed. I was very shocked by this news and Dahlke told me to go to a nearby house. In this house were around 10 wounded Kameraden. The room was filled with a very bad smell and almost every soldier in there had been shot in the stomach. There was no doctor or first-aiders there, so the situation was very difficult. I used the plentiful snow to cool their heads and wet their lips. In the darkness a hand took my arm and a voice asked me to shoot them. This request was repeated again and again and I will never forget the sound of this voice. I can only assume that this soldier died shortly afterwards as he stopped asking me whilst I held his hand. I took part in the continuing attack of the 3.Kompanie the following morning. I took control of the re-connected telephone contact to you in the evening. The fighting continued over the following day and the battle was hard and heavy, but we succeeded in securing the whole of Bereka by then. This is how I recall the time of your 30th birthday (16th February 1943). Sixty years have passed, but the memories of those days are like yesterday!"*. Gunther Zaag recalled that the quantity of men

SS-Untersturmfuhrer **Gunther Zaag.**

Albert Frey shown in March 1943 after his award of the Knight's Cross.

that the *3.Kompanie* had, were insufficient to cover the ground that they were assigned. He did however, recall that they were confident of victory, as they had the element of surprise. Besides the usual K98 rifles and MP40s, they were backed up with one heavy mortar and a heavy machine-gun. As the days moved towards the Bereka fight, Zaag witnessed the loss of many of this kameraden, including one of the men standing right next to him, cut down by machine-gun fire; Zaag suffered a bread bag full of holes! Just prior to the Bereka fight, the *3.Kompanie* had 60 men in their order of battle. Besides the enemy in front of them, they had waist-deep snow and temperatures of -25 degrees to contend with. On the morning of the attack itself, *SS-Untersturmführer* Hans Flocke was shot through the head by a sniper's bullet, walking next to Zaag. The situation became confused very quickly, with further officers and man falling to the increasingly heavy enemy fire from bullets and mortars; the element of surprise belonged to the Soviets! It was during this confusion that Hermann Dahlke took control and led the remaining men to an effective outcome, until they were relieved. Both Hermann Dahlke and Gunther Zaag reported to their Battalion Commander, Albert Frey the day following their relief. Both soldiers found it very difficult to recount the actions that had taken place at Bereka and the impact upon their *3.Kompanie*. Zaag recalled the pale complexion of Albert Frey, as they recounted what had taken place. Besides the award of the Knight's Cross to both Albert Frey and Hermann Dahlke, Zaag and Dahlke would be promoted to the rank of *SS-Untersturmführer* during early March.

Albert Frey, March 1943.

Zaag received the First Class Iron Cross. Hermann Dahlke's was a field promotion and he was also given the command of the *3.Kompanie*. He held that position until the 5th of July 1943, when he was killed on the first day of the Kursk offensive. Gunther Zaag assumed field command of that *Kompanie* for the remaining Kursk battles. Albert Frey was promoted to *SS-Obersturmbannführer* on the 21st of June and also given command of the *SS-Panzer Grenadier Regiment 1*, following the reorganization of the *LAH* prior to Kursk. He led his *Regiment* during the difficult Kursk battles, seeing some of his men recognized for their bravery, but also losing the likes of Knight's Cross holder, Hermann Dahlke. He went into Italy in the second half of the year and Gunther Zaag was alongside Albert Frey then, performing the function of Ordnance Officer for the *I.Battalion*. Frey led the surrender negotiations for the city of Milan, with Zaag being part of that negotiation team who discussed the terms with the Italian General Vittorio Ruggero, the outcome was a surrender without a fight. Gunther Zaag went to on be awarded the German Cross in Gold, in May 1944, for actions stretching back to Kharkov and Kursk; he was captured in the fighting in Aachen in late-1944.

Albert Frey with Theodore Wisch and Rudolf Lehmann.

Jochen Peiper and Albert Frey.

Albert Frey and his men returned to southern Russia in November. Thrown into the intensive battles at that time, he conducted actions that resulted in him being recommended for the Oakleaves to his existing Knights Cross by his Divisional Commander, Teddi Wisch on the 16th of December. An overview is as follows: "*1. With the Operation 'Zitadelle' on 5.7.1943 the Commander of the* SS-Panzer-Grenadier-Regiments 1,

SS-Obersturmbannführer *Frey, had the order, after removing the combat posts on the heights west of Jachontoff with his Regiment, to take the tank ditch near Hill 220.5 and thereby the main road to the place Jakolewo under his control. Under the heaviest hostile artillery fire, the infantry stormed from their jump-off points and worked themselves close to the tank ditch by using fully the ground around them. They suffered heavy losses from the extraordinarily violent fire coming from the enemy, who were sat in deep and well constructed trench systems. The tank ditch was nevertheless taken during a five-hour fight, with attack-troops assisting here. Since the tank ditch and the ground to the north of there was heavily mined and covered with wire, plus the accurate effect of the hostile artillery, also to the north, the threat of the attack stalling, existed.*

Waffen-SS grenadiers in a tank ditch on the Kursk front, Summer 1943 (U.S. Nat. Archives).

SS grenadier with a MG-42.

SS-Obersturmbannführer *Frey immediately recognized this crisis during this attack day, gathering a handful of Pioneers together, he blew a lane through the tank ditch and created with this, an advance route over this for the tanks. Moving at the same time as the armour, he advanced through and personally led his infantry forward and once again managed to get the attack rolling again. We are to thank the resolution, the personal employment in the foremost line and outstanding bravery of SS-Obersturmbannführer Frey for the fact that the entire attack of the Division moved over and beyond the tank ditch. Not remaining there, during this day and the next, a deep advance was made through the mined and wire entangled positions on Hill 243.2 and in a close struggle around each dug-in enemy position, the daily objective of Hill 230.5 could finally be taken.*

2. With the attack of the 1.SS-Panzer-Division 'LSSAH', from the 15.11 until the 18.11.1943, into the deep flank of the enemy, who had penetrated out of Kiev upon Shitomir. SS-Obersturmbannführer Frey had an armoured group (Panther-Abteilung, Stu.Gesch.Abt, II./Art.Rgt. and his SS-Panz.Gren.Rgt. 1) and was given the order to breakthrough Kornin from the north and advance on Ssolowjewka and from there, move northwest up to the main road Kiev-Shitomir and close this road. The armoured group started to advance from Kornin towards Ssolowjewka at 06:30 hours in the morning of the 15.11.1943. After the Panther-Abteilung and the Stu.Gesch.Abt. provided support against a

Pakfront *on the ground south of the village of Lissowka, where well-disciplined* T-34 *also joined the fight, the remainder of the Regiment advanced, despite the heaviest flanking artillery and more anti-tank fire, upon Lissowka and took this place. SS-Obersturmbannführer Frey was at the foremost advance line after Lissowka had been penetrated and pushed through this place, regrouping his Regiment in the shortest possible time, then advanced further after ordering a combined burst of fire from all of the combined heavy weapons and artillery.*

A *StuG.III* of the *Leibstandarte*, on the Kursk front.

SS-Grenadier, 1943.

Waffen-SS Grenadier at Kursk.

He personally led his foremost Battalion in the drive upon Ssolowjewka. This village contained enemy, those who had not been already met by the Division, who had also not noticed that a flanking movement westwards from Fastow had taken place. This place developed into a cornerstone of the developing defensive front. After the artillery had given a burst of fire and after close combat with one Pakfront *to the south of this place, a* Panther *set off to the northwest of this place, during which SS-Ostubaf. broke into this place from the south. This village was fought through in the shortest time and all resistance was broken. With the reserve Battalion and the Stu.Gesch.Abt., SS-Ostubaf. Frey stormed after the retreating enemy to the northwest and was able the following night, to break the enemy resistance in Wodoty, Pokryschew, Romanowka, Semmewka and Sdwischka. This was after a surprise night attack, in which, once again, the personal leadership and outstanding bravery of SS-Ostubaf. Frey is to be thanked* for the advance into Wilnja. During the night of the 16. through to the 17.11.1943, the Kampfgruppe *in Wilnja began to move further northwards. His initial pursuing attack was towards the direction of Korostyjew, which SS-Obersturmbannführer Frey reached during dawn with his foremost advance. They came parralel to the main road and the edge of the forest and found these to be strongly occupied by the enemy. After personal investigation, he had the impression that the enemy had succeeded, in the shortest time, along to their initial attack goal.*

SS-Ostubaf. **Albert Frey, showing his Ritterkreuz with Oakleaves.**

Sepp Dietrich, Theodore Wisch and Albert Frey on the occasion of Dietrich's 50th birthday.

He decided to turn after this to the northeast and to take control of the area Kotscherowo, lying between them. Since he depended on the main road to close up as fast as possible, he set in motion his resolution to move out immediately. He attacked the Russians for control of this extraordinarily important road junction and by noon, had this firmly in his hands. The blocking of the main road was made possible due to his independent resolution and decision to attack without any time delay!

On the 18.11.1943, SS-Obersturmbannführer *Frey with his* Kampfgruppe, *had to stop their continued march due to the bottomless roads, the large night fighting which had been extraordinarily hard, and by the grey morning up to 16:00 hours, had to repel 8 attacks by the enemy who were between Battalion - Regimental strength, with armour support. All of these attacks were stubborn, since the Russians wanted to keep the road open from Shitomir under all circumstances. They were repulsed however, with high enemy losses. Many of our own Kompanies had themselves fallen, since the enemy tanks had gone around and threatened our flank until they broke back into the houses in this village. In each case however, we took them back only by using all of our available forces upon this weak enemy. The personal leadership of* SS-Obersturmbannführer *Frey is to be emphasized and thanked for keeping the men alive and for the failure of this enemy attack.*

I hold that SS-Ostubaf. *Frey, due to his outstanding leadership of his Regiment and his proven personal bravery in all of the battle days, is worthy of the honour of the award of the Oakleaves to the Knight's Cross to the Iron Cross and please ask that he be awarded this".*

This recommendation was approved very rapidly and only four days later, on the 20th of December, Albert Frey became the fourth Oakleaves holder for the *Leibstandarte*. Frey remained with the *LAH* as they fought into 1944 in Russia then moved westwards once again in mid-1944. He received a heavy wound from a grenade splinter in the Normandy fighting, on the 20th of July, which removed him from the front-line. He was promoted to *SS-Standartenführer* and his file lists him as being on the Reserve Officer list from this time. There are various sources that list a variety of posts and functions that were held by Albert Frey until the conclusion of the war, but none can be verified. His files lists the reserve officer status until then. In the post-war years and he helped to form the veterans association of the *LAH*.

Albert Frey in late-June 1944, in Mouen, Normandy.

Albert Frey and Wisch.

Albert Frey and myself at his home in May 2000.

He was the First Speaker of this organization until his health prevented him from attending the re-unions anymore. I had the opportunity to meet with Albert Frey and his wife at their home in May 2000, whilst attending the reunion of the *I.SS-Panzer Korps*. He was a very hospitable and amenable person. He was one of three former *Leibstandarte* soldiers that left a deep impression upon me, the other two being Heinrich Springer and Otto Gunsche. On the 1st of September 2003, Albert Frey shot his terminally ill wife and then shot himself straight after. They had been together since the war and this final act of mercy for his wife is a testament to his resolve and personal convictions.

Bibliography

Peter Mooney, "*Dietrich's Warriors – The History of the 3.Kompanie / Ist Panzergrenadier Regiment, 1st SS-Panzer Regiment Leibstandarte SS-Adolf Hitler in World War II*", Schiffer Publishing, 2004

Peter Mooney, "*Waffen-SS Knights and Their Battles – Volume 2 (January to July 1943)*", Schiffer Publishing, 2010

Peter Mooney, "*Waffen-SS Knights and Their Battles – Volume 3 (August to December 1943)*", Schiffer Publishing, 2012

Personal recollections of Gunther Zaag, privately published

Personal discussions and correspondence with Albert Frey, Gerhard Dilling and myself (2000– 2004)

Photographs are from various sources including my own archive, the *Bundesarchiv* and other privately owned archives.

The French Legion through the eyes of an SS-Kriegsberichter
Belarus, summer 1943
by Chris Chatelet

Present from the winter 1941 on the Eastern front, as the 638th Regiment of the German army, the L.V.F. (*Légion des Volontaires Français contre le bolchevisme*) was engaged in the rear of the front, in the areas infested by the Soviet partisans, of the Army Group Center. At the end of June, a team of war correspondents, composed of three German cameramen and a photographer *SS-Kriegsberichter*, arrived in Belynitschi (35 kilometers west of Mohilev), where the command post of the *III.Bataillon* was located, attached administratively to the 286th Security Division (*286.Sicherungs-Division*) under the orders of the *Generalleutnant* Johann-Georg Richert (command post at Orscha). The commander, Eugène Panné, Saint-Cyrien, a veteran officer of the colonial army, who had enlisted on August 1, 1942 and who had been at the head of the battalion since January 28, 1943, chose his 11th Company to serve as a model for the Germans of this Propaganda-Kompanie.

The *Leutnant* Seveau (from behind) interrogates an old farmer. On his left, the *Oberleutnant* Audibert, which has its regiment number (638) on its shoulder tabs. On the right, a *Waffen SS* with glasses, observes the scene.

A patrol sent to an area infested by the partisans across the road from Mohilev, was committed to providing material to the filmmakers, since the French were sure to clash with the enemy. Two fighting platoons were engaged: the first of the *Oberleutnant* Roger

Audibert, who arrived on May 15 in Russia at the age of 29 and the 3rd Platoon under the orders of *Leutnant* Jacques Seveau, enlisted from 1941 in the Légion.

Same characters during the interrogation. Note that Seveau has taken off his officer's cap. The soldier on the left is carrying a crossed belt of a hundred cartridges which is also passed under his belt, despite the fact that the *MG-34* would jam with the cartridges improperly loaded in the belt and with bent links.

The propaganda film with the men of the 11th Company, with the photos taken by Weis, where the legionaries had to pretend, became in reality a real fight.

These two platoons had to defend a position along a tributary of the Dnieper on which a bridge passed a dozen miles to the left of Mohilev, a little before the 11th Company, settled further west and from which they had been posted. With the help of requisitioned carts, on which their weapons were loaded, especially the *MG-34* and ammunition, the troop headed to a village where, according to information recovered, especially from the local population, strong enemy grouping was operating. It was decided to deploy on the ground at the entrance of the village, after some sentinels who were present had fled escape the legionaries who were advancing on the road. Only one Bolshevik was killed just before the village entrance which was then inspected, but it was empty because the alarm had been sounded.

In front of an isba in flames, the French all move forward, like the men of PK, who follow the action at the risk of their own lives, to capture the images.

Sergeant Yvan de Rodellec du Portzic, his back with his *MP-40* submachine gun, in the stormed village. He did not survive the Russian campaign, because he fell in combat the following year, March 30, 1944.

The return trip turned out to be difficult, since fire from automatic weapons immediately came from the nearby forest, where the 'reds' had set up an ambush position. However, in the face of the resolute advance of the legionaries towards the forest under the heavy fire of the partisans, they abandoned the fight, taking with them their fallen and their wounded. Being accustomed to the front lines, the team of war correspondents immortalized everything on the film. For his part, NCO Weis, SS-PK, took numerous photos, shown in this article, made during the return of the patrol to its positions, including the inspection of a village along the road that witnessed the legionaries seeking information on the local population.

The sergeant de Rodellec du Portzic, behind the horseman, surrounds a suspect with his men, after having cleared out the houses. The Legionaries because of the strong heat, do not wear caps.

The letters L.V.F., sewn on his national shield that the French wore on his right shoulder, this legionnaire asks a peasant to know where the enemy is.

In the end, this combat action, in addition to its function as propaganda, made a positive contribution, by fending off for a brief time a group of partisans and therefore to provide a small degree of security for the positions held by the legionaries.

Thanks to the film shot by the cameramen, in these four frames, we can see the photographer Weis, on the right with the camera and the binoculars.

Frame of the film with a legionnaire with an *MG-34*.   **Some frames of the *'Fort Cambronne'*.**

It should be noted that a part of the filmed images was used to make a propaganda film, which came out in France under the title of *'Fort Cambronne'* and which told the life of the two battalions of the anti-Bolshevik French Legion on the Eastern front.

The photos in the article come from Chris Chatelet's personal collection.

Free Corps Denmark at Velikije Luki
by Lars Larsen

After the most discussed leave of absence of Free Corps Denmark, they travelled from Copenhagen to Mitau in Latvia. Free Corps Denmark stayed here until the middle of November 1942, where after it was transferred to the town of Bobruisk in current Belarus. In Mitau, Free Corps Denmark got educated and received practical training for winter war. The idea was that Free Corps Denmark should be deployed to combat partisans in Belarus. Free Corps Denmark was assigned to 1st SS-Brigade, which was infamous for their brutal combat against partisans. On the 19/11/1942, when major Russian forces attacked, all of this changed. After this, Free Corps Denmark was sent to the front instead of combatting partisans. The Russians attacked around the town of Velikije Luki.

Positions of *Frikorps* in the Velikiye-Luki area, 1942-1943.

German defensive position.

Danish volunteers committed to downloading materials.

The Russians hoped that this attack would drive in a wedge between the German Army Group North and Army Group South. The purpose of the attack was to try to cut off the whole of the middle and northern part of the German front and press them against the Baltic. The Germans faced a grave situation, as a Russian breakthrough would cause the Germans to lose control of the middle and northern part. During this attack, the Russians trapped about 7500 Germans soldiers in the town of Velikije Luki. On the 5/12/1942, Free Corps Denmark arrived with a force of approximately 1100 soldiers to the town of Nevel, southwest of Velikije Luki. After a couple of days, the different companies were brought to the frontline. Free Corps Denmark had to defend a part of a very thinly fortified frontline, which was the place of the railroads between the towns of Velikije Luki and Nevel. The companies of Free Corps Denmark were deployed north of the town of Bobrikowo, where they had to cover an area of 5 kilometers.

A group of Danish volunteers on the Velikije Luki front.

Hstuf. Neergard-Jacobsen.

A Danish volunteer on the Eastern front.

This meant that each company should cover an area of about 1,5 kilometers. The positions of Free Corps Denmark consisted of small bunkers, which was connected by paths through the huge masses of snow. On several occasions, however, the Russians managed to get through the relatively thin and undefended German defense lines. Continuously, Free Corps Denmark sent out patrols to the undefended lines, which resulted in minor battles with the Russians, which resulted in killed and wounded. Unlike the summer effort in the Demyansk- Pocket, snow and temperature down to minus 30 degrees marked the battlefield. As the cold got worse, more cold related injuries happened. Louse and skin rashes as well as the stay in the cold bunkers were major problems for the soldiers of Free Corps Denmark. On the 19/12/1942, Free Corps Denmark shifted their position, so they moved to the west, to the towns of Laskaturino, Kondratowo and Taidy. Since Free Corps Denmark re-deployed to the front, they had only experienced few and short battles against the Russian forces. However, Free Corpse Denmark was to participate in two major battles against the Russians. The first was on Christmas Eve in 1942.

Danish volunteers on the Velikije Luki front, January 1943.

A Danish defensive position, with a *MG-34*.

German artillery on the Velikije Luki front, 1943.

The second major battle – The town of Taidy

After the battles of the Christmas days in 1942, that part of the front was relatively quiet. The small town of Taidy, which the Russians had occupied for a while, was a major nuisance for the Germans. Therefore, it was decided that a major attack should be launched at the town in February in 1943. Taidy was situated at a relatively high place, from which the Russians had a good view of the area, including the railroad between Velikije Luki and Nevel. The town had been rebuilt by the Russians to a complete fortress, which contained many underground passages, tunnels as well as observation posts for the Russian artillery. Commanded by *Ostuf.*, Heinz Henneke, a German, the Germans should defeat the Russians at their positions. The attack was a success. Afterwards, the pioneer platoon of Free Corps Denmark blew up the fortress. The remaining time at the front, until the 20/3/1943, was relatively quiet. From that date, Free Corps Denmark started withdrawing its soldier from the frontline area, and four days later, it was left for 1st SS-Brigade. After this, Free Corps Denmark was sent to Grafenwöhr barrack in southern Germany by train. The total loss of the unit was 44 soldiers and an unknown number of wounded in the winter war of Velikije Luki.

Jens Pank Bjerregaard, Lars Larsen

Danish Volunteers of the Waffen-SS: Freikorps Danmark 1941-43
Helion and Company

Danish Volunteers of the Waffen-SS tells the story of Freikorps Danmark in pictures from 1941-1943. Freikorps Danmark was established as a Danish corps to fight communism and, from its beginning, was controlled from Denmark, being placed under the control of the SS-Division Totenkopf and 1.SS-Brigade during its service on the Eastern Front. The source material for this book has been gathered from the photo collections of former members of the unit and includes a large number of previously unpublished images.

Hungarian Armored Forces in WW2
by Eduardo Manuel Gil Martínez
(Translated by José Antonio Muñoz Molero) – 2nd part

One of the few *Marder II* who where used in Hungary as a loan. Its formidable firepower represented an important improvement within the Magyar armoured forces. Courtesy of Károly Németh.

A *PzKpfw 38(t)* of the 1st Armored Division, 1943.

Hungarian troops, February 1943.

1943. Disaster and reorganization

On January 2, the 1st Armoured Division was subordinated to the Cramer Group which was the only reserve unit of the Army Group B. The Cramer Group was constituted by the German Divisions 26th and 168th, the 190 cannons of assault detachment and 700 German armoured detachment. On January 6, the Hungarians received in loan five *Marder II*; these tank hunters were integrated into a new unit called the 1st Independent tank hunter company. Towards January 7, the Hungarians counted on 16 Pz IV (8 short barreled and 8 long barreled), 41 Pz 38, two 38M Toldi I, 5 *Marder*, some 40M Nimrod and 9 Pz III M. But this calm situation was about to change as on January 12, 1943 there was a powerful Soviet attack against the line of the front maintained by the rather weakened Hungarian troops from Uryv, Schutschye and Kantemirovka. The confusion was total as many units lacked even their proper armament and ammunition, so the only thing the Hungarian veteran troops could do was to resist the hell that broke out before them. The counter-attack of the 1st Hungarian Armoured Division took place finally on January 16, after receiving the order to try to seal the gaps that were remaining in the defensive line and to support the withdrawal of the

Hungarian troops. On the 17th afternoon, the Hungarian Armoured Division made a counterattack with 8 PZ III and 4 Pz IV towards Dolschik-Ostrogosshk destroying a column of Soviet vehicles. That day the division lost a lot of material that had to be left behind and be blown away by lack of fuel and breaks and mechanical problems. The Pz 38 were totally useless with the snow so deep and the temperatures so extreme; Battalion 30/I had to blown up at least 17 Pz 38, 2 Pz IV and other vehicles because they could not take them with them during the retreat. On January 18, the mission of the Armoured Division was to attack and retake Alekseyevka supported by the 559th German tank hunter detachment that was subordinated to it. After two and a half hours of combat, the city was reconquered, but the next day it was abandoned after a new Soviet attack.

German Pz IV H tanks fought alongside the Hungarian troops at River Don , January 1943.

German Pz IV H at River Don , January 1943.

After several days of combat, on the 27th of January, the 2nd Hungarian Army was almost annihilated. The last important combats took place on February 7th;then on February 9th, the Armoured Division crossed the Donetz River, reaching Charkow and definitively withdrawing from the front line. At this time the only armoured vehicles left to the Hungarian unit were two *Marder*.

Armoured vehicles in the occupation troops

We must not forget the Hungarian troops that were in the rear, doing their job, as they also had their armoured park. They were constituted in 1942: the Tank Independent Squa-

Several French-made *H-39 Hotchkiss* arranged alongside anti-aircraft in second-line positions. All of these vehicles were lost in the antipartisan operations (*Károly Németh*).

March 1944: units of the *16.SS-Pz.Gren.Div.* enter Budapest.

A *Turan I* tank advances by a combat zone. On the side of the road you will appreciate Hungarian troops taking a break.

drons 101º and 102º (the 103º cannot be confirmed to exist according to the existing reports currently), which took part supporting the Antipartisan activities of the Hungarians in territory Ukrainian. The 101st had received French combat tanks from the loot of war captured in France by the German: two *Somua S-35* who acted as command vehicles and 15 *Hotchkiss H-35/h-39*; the 102nd used vehicles of Hungarian manufacture. All these tanks of French origin were gradually lost in the period between 1942-1944 for various causes: attacks of partisans or of Soviet regular troops and in some cases destroyed by their own crews not being able to retreat with them, thus preventing them from falling intact into enemy hands.

1944. The beginning of the end

After the practice of destruction of the 1st Armoured Division at the Eastern Front in 1943, in 1944 began the task of rebuilding it; while a new armoured training unit was created that became the 2nd Armoured Division. The beginning of the year 1944 was not very hard for Hungary, but the second half of the year 1944 will become a real hell.

German troops in Budapest, March 1944.

The crossing of a river by a *Turan II* causes curiosity among several Magyar soldiers in a pause during the fighting in Galitzia in 1944. Courtesy of Károly Németh.

A Hungarian assault gun *43M Zrinyi II.*

After the Stalingrad disaster in February 1943, the demoralized Hungarian troops reconsidered the viability of their alliance with the Germans. The absence of a strong control over the Hungarian troops and the movements thereof, did not like in the High German HQ. This whole situation finally led to the Germans ocupy the "Allied" Hungary on March 19, 1944 in the so-called *"Margarethe"* operation. The German troops coming from neighbouring Austria and also from Croatia entered peacefully in Hungary to deploy in the Hungarian territory, although without surpassing the Tisza River where the 1st Hungarian Army was deployed at that time, to avoid any kind of clash. It would be from the German *"occupation"* when Hungary can finally mobilize its troops in a complete way, taking into service the 1st, 2nd and 3rd Armies; being the 1st and 2nd Armoured Divisions subordinated to them.

Fighting for Galitzia

Due to the dazzling Soviet advance that was already in the westernmost areas of Ukraine, in the spring of 1944 the 1st Hungarian Army moved from the Carpathians to the region of Galitzia stabilizing the situation between the Ukraine-North and Ukraine- South German Armies Groups along the line Kolomea-Ottyina-Stanislavov. The 2nd Armoured Division (belonging to the 1st Army) which was the most powerful unit within the entire Hungarian Army was mobilized on March 13.

A *Turan I* crosses a busted bridge, 1944.

A *Turan I* during the fighting in Galitzia in 1944.

All the armored vehicles of the 2nd Armoured Division was from Hungarian origin: the 40M and 41 Turan, 40M Nimrod, 39M Csaba and 38M Toldi. The 2nd Armoured Division had 120 medium combat tanks Turan, 55 heavy combat tanks Turan, 84 light tanks Toldi (47 of them were armed with cannons of 40 mm), 42 anti-aircraft Nimrod and 14 Csaba. As a negative point, the Division did not have maintenance units that would allow them to have combat tanks under proper operating conditions. Between 5 and 11 April 1944, the 2nd Hungarian Armoured Division, under the command of Colonel Osztovics, reached its meeting area in Stryj. From there they had to travel between 250 and 300 kilometers by their own means to the line of the front, advancing in muddy terrain with roads in bad snow covered. Once arrived at the front, they were deployed in a sector of about 60-70 kilometers, for what the Division was divided into two Combat Groups.

Another unit also assigned to the 1st Hungarian Army was the 1st Assault Tank Battalion under the command of Captain Barankay (a veteran from 1942 campaigns), whose main material was the brand new assault howitzer of Hungarian manufacture: Zrínyi. The 2nd and 3rd batteries of the Battalion departed to the front on the 12th of April, arriving on the 16th of the same month. The first mission of the 2nd Armoured Division took place between 17-19 April, together with German troops. The 2nd Armoured Division launched an attack from Solotwina to Nadvorna, Delatyn and Kolomea, receiving support from German combat armoured (15 Marder from 615th Tank Hunter Battalion, 7 Pz IV and 7-9 Tiger from 503rd Panzer Battalion). Nadvorna and Delatyn were captured on 18 April, after intense fighting which allowed establishing two bridgeheads on the river Bistrica banks.

Hungarian Zrínyi Assault gun.

Ervin Tarczay poses over his *Pz VI Tiger* in this frontal view. Commanding this vehicle he got many of his victories in multiple clashes. June 1944 (*Károly Németh*).

An Hungarian *Tiger I* tank, 1944.

The first prototype of the *Zrínyi II* was made of steel. Courtesy of Péter Mujzer.

The 1st Hungarian Army had achieved its goal of establishing the connection between the two of German Army Groups although these battles left completely in evidence the *Turan*, because a *T-34* could shoot them with probability of destroying them from 1500-2000 meters away, while for the same the Turan were to approach 600 meters in the case of porting a cannon of 75 mm or to 400 meters in the case of carrying a cannon of 40 mm.

For this reason, the German High command agreed on May 4th with the Hungarian government to partially reequip with German material to the 2nd Armoured Division. So, from 6 to 14 May, 12 Pz IV H, 10 Pz VI E Tiger, and 10 StuG III G, were delivered in Nadvorna. Battalion 3/I was equipped with German material, while Battalion 3/II was with the Hungarian Turans. After the reequipping, the Battalion 3/I had 4 companies, the 1st with 11 Pz IV H, the 2nd with 6 Tiger, the 3rd with 6 Tiger and the 4th with 9 StuG III. One of the companies that possessed the mighty Tiger was commanded by 1st Lieutenant Ervin Tarczay and the other one by Captain János Vetress. The surplus vehicles left by the various companies were delivered to the Division's 3/II Battalion in turn. In addition to the 10 Tiger received, the Germans gave away another 3 more. Besides a training unit was created for the new German material and it possessed one Tiger, one Pz IV H and one StuG III. Thanks to the arrival of new Zrínyi from the factories, the new Assault Tank Battalions began to be empowered; forming the 7th Assault Tank Battalion in Sümeg, the 10th in Szigetvár, the 13th in Csongrád, the 16th in Debrecen, the 20th in Eger, the 24th in Kassa and the 25th in Kolozsvár. In spite of which, there was no Zrínyi to complete all, so many times they continued using Toldi and Turan. In mid-June finally the 1st Battery of the 1st Assault Tank Battalion under the command of the first Lieutenant Sandor, came to the front coming from Hajmáskér with 10 Zrínyi, so it was the first time that all the 1st Assault Tank Battalion was fully equipped on the combat front (10 vehicles per battery and one command Zrínyi). On July 13rd, the Soviet Army launched an offensive towards Sandomierz and Lviv causing the break of the frontline defended by the Hungarians.

A *Toldi* tank in eastern Poland, Summer 1944.

A Hungarian *Flak*, 1944.

The Toldi IIa tank only represented a small improvement over the Toldi II, still very far from what the Magyar armored force required. Courtesy of Károly Németh.

The 1st Ukrainian Front under the command of Mariscal Koniev acted as a ram against the weak defensive lines of the axis, which were integrated by the *Heeresgruppe Nordukraine* that comprised the 4th Panzer Army in the left flank, the 1st Panzer Army in the center and the 1st Hungarian Army on the right flank. Because of this motive, the 2nd Armoured Division was put on alert and deployed with urgency in Stanislau on July 23, while the rest of the 1st Hungarian Army took shelter in the Carpathians where they would take positions in the incomplete fortifications of the line "*Hunyadi* ".

During the Soviet offensive in July, the 1st Assault Tank Battalion suffered many casualties, which motivated the 1st and 2nd batteries to be used as rear units to slow the Soviet advance to the east of Ottynia. The massive Soviet attack motivated the 1st Hungarian Army to definitively order the withdrawal of these troops, ordering the Tiger to act as the rear of that retreat. From the 24th to the 29th of July, the tanks belonging to the 2nd Armoured Division maintained

In this picture of Tarczay commanding his Tiger we can appreciate both the German emblem in the combat tank as its numeral, belonging to 2nd Armoured Division. Picture taken in Galitzia in June 1944. Courtesy of Károly Németh.

continuous clashes against the Soviets along the route Czuczylow-Grabevjec-Horohodina-Saturnia-Rosulna-Kraszna-Rozniatow-Dolina. These continuous clashes motivated the number of tanks in service to decrease dramatically, serving as an example Battalion 3/I that lost seven Tiger in the combats, only arriving to Hungarian territory three of them.

Side image of a Zrínyi II where we can clearly see the emblem with the white cross over black square which used most of the war the Magyar armoured troops. Courtesy of Károly Németh.

In these battles was forged the legend of Ervin Tarczay, the ace of the Hungarian armoured, in command of a Tiger. At the end of July, also the Zrínyi of the 1st Assault Tank Battalion had to withstand hard clashes with the Soviets to keep open the escape route of the troops in retreat in the valley of Lukwa, in direction Rozniatow, Dolina and finally Wygoda. The 1st and 2nd batteries suffered numerous casualties during this operation, reaching on July 28th the Hungarian border through the passage of Toronya in the Northeast zone of the Carpathians along with the staff of the 1st Assault Tank Battalion. The very worn out 2nd Armoured Division motivated the decision to be removed from the first line of combat to reorganize it in Huszt. By August 9 The arsenal of the 2nd Armoured Division was 14 Toldis, 40 Turan-40, 14 Turan-75, 1 Panzer III, 1 StuG III G and 9 Pz IV H. They had also survived after these combats 3 Tiger, but they were damaged enough to would remove them for later repair. Thanks to the positioning of the Hungarian troops in the Carpathians and the difficulties that this posed to the Soviet troops, a brief pause was achieved in the offensive.

A Turan II with Infantry soldiers aboard, is passing through a Hungarian village, August 1944.

The Zrinyi II had a 105 mm Howitzer.

On August 11, the Soviets again attacked the men belonging to 1st Hungarian Army. Although it would not be the Soviets the only concern of Hungary, since on August 25, Romania changed sides after a coup d'etat to then declare the war to its Hungarian neighbor and finally joined their troops with the Soviets in the attack for the taking of Transylvania. Faced with this new risk from the south, it was quickly organized and mobilized a new 2nd Army with two divisions, a reserve brigade, as well as three divisions that arrived from the East to which would be added the 2nd Armoured Division; as well as a weak 3rd Army. Simultaneously, the Soviet forces faced with the "*Hunyadi*" line in the Carpathians front, managed to break the defensive framework and penetrated into Hungarian territory on September 27, facing the "*St. László*" and "*Árpád*" defensive lines. Whereas by the north of Hungary, the Soviets tried to force the passage of Dukla (on the border with Slovakia). In the upcoming fight in Transylvania, the 10th Assault Tank Battalion would take part, the armoured Trains 101st and 102nd, in addition to the 2nd Armoured Division that only had 14 Toldi, 40 40M Turan 40, 14 41M Turan 75, 21 40M Nimrod and 12 39 Csaba , a Pz III, 9 Pz IV H, 3 Tiger and a StuG III. On September 20, it was agreed with the German Reich the dispatch of 20 Pz IV H and 5 Panther (the total of Panther which arrived in Hungarian hands was of 10-12), which were assigned to the company commanded by the first Lieutenant Tarczay into the 3/I Battalion.

Several Hungarian soldiers observe a Panther tank with curiosity. It is not known whether this vehicle belonged to the Germans or the Magyars. There are no known photos of a Panther tank with Magyar crews. Courtesy of Károly Németh.

The Tiger of the first Lieutenant Tarczay, 1944.

The Battle of Turda

On 5 September 1944, the Hungarians launched an offensive against superior Romanian forces aiming at the north of Transylvania. The spearhead was the 2nd Armoured Division and within it the powerful 2nd Company commanded by Tarczay. They departed after crossing the Aranyos River (Aries River) towards Turda at dusk in 5 September beginning the Magyar attack. The beginning of the Magyar offensive was a success since it was achieved to reach the locality of Torda (Turda, today in Romania) ten days after beginning and finally crossing the river Maros (Mures). But Romanian infantry troops joined to Soviet troops and the Romanian Armoured Division definitively stopped the Hungarians on 9 September in their attempt to reach the northern mountain passes in Transylvania. The numerical superiority of the Romanian troops was shown by blocking the Hungarian advance, which provoked the Hungarian refolding behind the Maros River where they would form a defensive line whose main bastions would be the populations of Torda and Aranyosegerbegy (Viişoara). On September 10th, the Magyar armoured troops were sent to the reserve, although three days later they returned to the front line (on September 13th) in Torda, where there was a strong Hungarian defensive line.

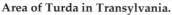

Area of Turda in Transylvania.

A Hungarian *PzKpfw.IV Ausf H* (K. Németh).

Hungarian soldiers on armored assault gun 43M Zrinyi II.

***Panther* in the Turda area, September 1944.**

Since then due to its strategic importance, the 2nd Armoured Division will be used as a mobile force ready to be sent to the neediest areas of the front. The Soviets during September 13th and 14th, managed to extend their offensive to the western part of the city. Meanwhile the Hungarian armoured troops were trying to plug the gaps that the Soviets created in their defensive system. On September 15th, the Soviets launched their first attack against the town of Torda after an intense artillery barrage. On the same day, the 3/I Battalion led by their Panther company made a successful counterattack. In particular the company led by Tarczay started this attack in the eastern area of Torda without waiting for the arrival of the rest of his battalion or infantry units, getting in this surprise maneuver destroy three anti-tank cannons and two enemy infantry companies. The overwhelming superiority of the enemy allowed Tarczay company to be surrounded but thanks to the valiant action of the Hungarian tanks they finally managed to avoid the siege. During the following days, there would be many fighting that would confront the armored Magyars against the Soviets, highlighting Tarczay with their Panthers. Also in the fighting for Torda, he highlighted the performance of the 10th Assault Artillery Battalion.

Not very good quality picture showing a *StuG.III* belonging to the 7th Assault Artillery Battalion in action. Courtesy of Károly Németh.

A Turan I of the 2nd Armored Division, September 1944.

A *Panther* on the Romanian front, Summer 1944.

It was the afternoon of September 22, when this unit launched a successful counterattack against the enemy that would surprise the Soviets, to later take advantage of the power of their cannons in short distances while in ambush positions. On September 23rd, in Vaskapu and Sósfar, in the east-northeast of Torda, the 23rd German Panzer Division arrived with two Panzergrenadier regiments and about 65 tanks. Thanks to this German troops, the sector was able to remain, allowing the retreating of the Axis troops involved in the combats around Torda. On September 24th, only 2 Panther, 6 Pz IV H and 9 Turan of the 3rd Tank Regiment remained in combat position, then they were sent to the reserve located in the town of Nagy-Ördöngös. On September 25th, the number of armoured in the reserve was increased upon receipt after its pertinent repairs 3 Panther and 3 Tiger, which were incorporated to their companies of origin. On 4 October, new Soviet attacks were repeated from the west, in such a way that at dusk they had almost completely completed the siege of Torda. The situation became desperate so that the troops of the Axis stationed in Transylvania had to retreat on 8 October. This retreat was used by the Romanians to capture Apahira (east of Kolozsvár) where they had a violent clash with the Hungarian armoured on 11 October. Between 15 September and 5 October 1944 in the Torda area, the Panther company destroyed 11 tanks, 17 anti-tank cannons, 20 machine guns, a rocket launcher and a lot of infantry troops. The Battle of Torda possibly meant the greatest operational success of the Magyar troops, as the ultimate goal of the Soviets and their Romanian allies was to encircle the largest number of troops on the axis to try to annihilate the Army Group South. The battle for the city of Torda allowed to retard this attempt and therefore to avoid it. The Battle of Torda had been a great 'carnage' for armoured troops between destroyed and captured vehicles.

Two Turan II captured by the Soviets being prepared for transport. Courtesy of Károly Németh.

Several Turan II ready to be transported to the USSR.

The Turan II with its 75 mm short gun represented almost the summit of the Magyar manufacture of combat tanks in the period of WW2 (*K.Németh*).

Concerning the latter, the Romanians captured several Toldi, Turan, two Hetzer and at least one Zrínyi. Continued fighting incessantly in Magyar territory, thus on 25 October Tarczay was struggling in the vicinity of Tiszapolgár, while the Magyar troops were in continuous retreat (their company destroyed between 6 and 25 October, 5 tanks).

Southern Hungary battles

After the defection of Romania, the 4th Hungarian Corp was organized to block the advance of the Soviet and Romanian forces in the plains of southern Hungary in Arad and Lippa. The 4th Hungarian Corp was added the VII Corp, being redesignated as III Army.

Two Nimród participating in an air-fire exercise. Some of the infants are relaxed and enjoying the show (*Németh*).

A Turan I on the Arad front, September 1944.

Hungarian armored units is entering in Arad, Sept. 1944.

A *StuG.III* with infantry aboard, Autumn 1944.

One of the constituent units of the 4th Hungarian Corp was the 1st Armoured Division, its most powerful unit. The 1st Armoured Division, was not at that time to the maximum of its theoretical capacity of armoured vehicles since part of its armament was to be handed over to the 2nd Armoured Division to complete that unit. The new unit was formed in August 1944, because the imminent need for its use in the front. On 2 September, the 1st Armoured Division had a tank battalion (1/III) with 5 Toldis in the command company, three medium-tank companies (with 7 Turan, 5 Toldi and 3 Nímrod per company); the 1st Motorized Riflemen Regiment had 9 Nímrod, while the 51st self-propelled anti-aircraft artillery Battalion had two command Toldis, 18 Nímrod and 3 Toldis. The 1st Armoured Division had about 60-70 armoured vehicles in September 1944. Due to pressures received by the Germans, on 13 September, the Hungarian troops made an attack advancing from the right flank of the front line from the region of Makó and Gyula towards Arad, but two Rumanian infantry divisions and one cavalry division were awaiting that advance. The commander of the Third Army required the 1st Armoured Division to support the infantry in this attack. The capture of Arad at dusk of September 13th, can be considered as the last completely independent operation of the Magyars during the Second World War. Between September 14th and 17th, the 1st Armoured Division fought against the 19th Romanian Infantry Division, breaking its defensive line by 16 September during 24 hours then they were slowed down due to Soviet armoured units. Despite this on 18 September, the Magyars had managed to reach the foothills of the Carpathians, but now a tenacious resistance of Romanian and Soviet troops slowed them down in their progress definitively. Then a counterattack carried out by a Soviet armoured Corp and 53 Soviet Army forced to retreat to the Magyars towards the line Dombegyháza-Battonya. In these clashes were lost between 23 vehicles *Turan* and *Toldi* by enemy fire.

Command tank of 1st Armoured Division, 1944.

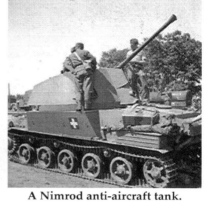

A Nimrod anti-aircraft tank.

German *StuG.III* and infantry on the Hungarian front.

A *T-34* destroyed on the Hungarian front, 1944.

On 20 September, a joint Soviet-Romanian attack supported by 40-50 tanks broke the Hungarian defensive line so the 1st Armoured Division had to go from the reserve to support its infantry. In the area of Lippa and Máriaradna the 1st Armoured Division supported a Hungarian counteroffensive with the support of the 7th Assault Artillery Battalion that had 18 *StuG III*; being also supported from the air by a German Group with Stukas. They all managed to destroy, in which it has been called the "*Pénzespuszta Tank Battle*", some 100 Soviet armoured vehicles between which there would be at least 28 *T-34*. The defensive structure in the southern Hungary fell in the Army Group South under the command of the general Johannes Friessner. This one counted with the II Hungarian Army (under command of General Jeno Major) where the 2nd Hungarian Armoured Division was inserted; the III Hungarian Army (under command of General József Heszlény) where the 1st Hungarian Armoured Division was included, and the VI German Army (under command of General Maximilian Fretter-Pico). By the 22 September, the Soviets had the vast Hungarian plain before their eyes. At 4.00 hours on 6 October, the 2nd Ukrainian Front began a major offensive to Hungary starting from the city of Arad supported by huge numbers of soldiers and armored vehicles to be distributed between the rivers Danube and Tisza. The advance was dazzling by not finding just opposition to it, allowing them to penetrate about 60 miles behind enemy lines during the first day. Of the

A German *Marder III* self-propelled gun passes Hungarian infantry, Autumn 1944 (*Ullstein Bilderdienst*).

many clashes between Soviets and defenders, it is worth highlighting the fighting in the Szentes bridgehead in October 1944, where among other units, was the 13th Assault Artillery Battalion with only two Turan 75. Despite the German resistance, on October 8 the Soviet troops crossed the natural border of Hungary on the Szegez sector. During the next few days, they would be the Panzer Divisions 1st , 13th and 23rd and the 22nd SS Cavalry Division "*Maria Theresa*", which managed to temporarily stop the Soviet advance. On October 11, began a counteroffensive of the Axis troops headed by the tanks of the 1st Armoured Division and the 23rd Hungarian Division, which allowed to overwhelm the Soviet vanguard in Mindszent, getting to destroy almost completely to the 4th Romanian Infantry Division. The Hungarian thrust was slowed on October 22 by mechanized Soviet forces, which in a backlash to the north of the Tisza River managed to push back the Magyars, leaving the free path towards Debrecen and Nyíregyháza. These battles had again bled the Hungarian troops, so trying to reorganize them, on October 29, 1944 the remains of the 1st Hungarian Armoured Division (with about 20 tanks ready to combat by 31 October) were under the command of the III German Panzer Corps in Kecskemét.

Bibliography

Csaba Becze, "*Magyar Steel*", Stratus. 2006.
Denes Bernád, Charles K. Kliment, "*Magyar warriors. The history of the Royal Hungarian Armed Forces 1919-1945. Volume I*", Helion & Company. 2015.
Denes Bernád, Charles K. Kliment, "*Magyar warriors. The history of the Royal Hungarian Armed Forces 1919-1945. Volume II*", Helion & Company. 2017.
Attila Bonhardt, "*Zrínyi II assault howitzer*", PeKo Publishing. 2015.
Eduardo Manuel Gil Martínez, "*Fuerzas acorazadas húngaras 1939-45*", Almena. 2017.
Peter Mujzer, "*Huns on wheels*", Mujzer&Partner Ltd.
Steven J. Zaloga, "*Tanks of Hitler´s eastern allies. 1941-45*", Osprey Publishing. 2013.

The Folgore Division
by Giuseppe Lundari

Grottaglie, 1942. An unit of the *Folgore* Division parading at the end of an exercise, just before the departure for North Africa. In front a 47/32 a/t gun.

General Enrico Frattini.

The *Folgore* Parachute Division under the covering name of 185th '*Cacciatori d'Africa*' Division was sent towards the Northern African front starting from middle July 1942, and occupyed the extreme Southern part of the Italo-German deployment, an area between Deir el Munassib at North and the Qaret el Himeimat heights at South bordering with the large Qattara depression. Its strenght included two Parachute Infantry Regiments, the 186th (three battalions: 5th, 6th and 7th) and the 187th (four battalions: 2nd, 4th, 9th and 10th; later on, due to the losses, the 10th battalion was disbanded its effectives joining the 9th battalion), the 185th Parachute Artillery Regiment (three 'groups': 1st, 2nd and 3rd, with 47/32 antitank guns), the 8th Parachute Guastatori battalion, regimental gun companies and divisional autonomous companies (81mm mortars, miners-engineers, signal) plus various services for a total of about 5,000 men. The units were distributed along the front line some at dependance of other units, placed in bordering areas, and went at once in action in the frame of a more general offensive of the Axis forces know as 'six days battle' or 'Alam Halfa'.

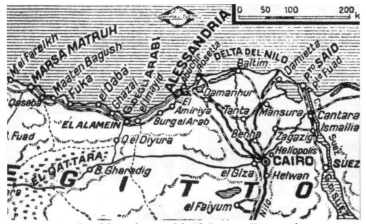

North African front with El Qattara Depression.

Italian soldiers at El-Alamein.

Paratroopers deployed along the Southern front.

Italian defensive position on the Southern front.

The attack that went on from 30 August to 3 September, did not reach the hoped results and Rommel was forced to order the withdrawal on the departure lines. For the *Folgore*, instead, the balance of the operation was fully positive, both for the particular operative successes (patrol attacks, coup de main in the thick of the enemy defences capturing prisoners, weapons and vehicles), and most of all for the behaviour of its men, who, tested in battle for the first time, showed to fully own those gifts of combativeness, courage and initiative that would render them famous.

By the start of September, the Division had reconstituted its own unity by the reentering of all units in its lines. Its deployment was articulated on four tactical group: *Ruspoli* (with 7th and 8th Pioneers battalions) at North, *Bechi* (2nd and 4th) and *Camosso* (9th and 10th) in the center, *Tantillo* (5th and 6th) at South. The three Artillery Groups, contracted to two (1st and 3rd) were assigned to the four tactical Groups with the task of advanced antitank defence. At the end of the month, the British tried to break in Deir el Munassib sector.

Italian mortar *Brixia* crew in action.

An Italian anti-tank artillery position.

English tanks move to the attack.

The paratroops stubborn defence vanished the attack and caused to the enemy large losses in men and vehicles. In this occasion, the Folgore's men sistematically adopted a tactic that, already used sporadically in the fighting at the end of August, gave good results and should reveal itself as their winning card in the future battle of El Alamein. It found its explication in the odds between Italians and British that were so disproportioned not to offer, in theory, the *Folgore* any hope of resistance to the enemy attacks. The British 8th Army had in fact deployed, in the southern sector, the *7th Armoured Division* (the famous *'Desert Rats'*, veteran of so many African battles) and three infantry Divisions, for a total strenght of about 50,000 men, with 400 guns, 350 tanks and 250 armoured vehicles. Ammunition, food and equipment stocks were pratically unlimited. On the other end, the Italians had about 3,500 paratroops, plus other 1,000 men not paratroops (31st Guastatori d'Africa battalion and an infantry battalion of the *Pavia* Division), about eighty artillery pieces, 5 tanks (German), no vehicles of their own, lack of ammunition and equipment, food in such low quantity and quality to cause serious illness to more than 30% of the force. To summarize, the odds were 1:13 for men, 1:5 for artillery, 1: 70 for tanks.

The *Folgore*, therefore, had only to count on the psychological factor, using the big morale gift of its men, strenght of spirit, ability to adapt themselves to the situation, tendency to mantain anyway the initiative, besides an extraordinary courage, never arriving to rashness, because the main preoccupation of the paratroops, from the commander to the last private, was always that to limit the losses at the minimum. The British attack tactics showed always the same characteristics of extreme adherence to the schemes studied at the table, that is, in other words, an initial strong opening fire and then, after the lenghtening of the fire, an advance at closed ranks of very strong infantry formations, often preceeded by tanks.

An anti-tank position of the *Folgore* on the North African front, Autumn 1942.

An Italian parachutist from the *Folgore* Division throws himself under the tracks of a British *Sherman* with his mine to blow it up (North Africa, 1942).

A *Folgore* 47/32 gun team, North Africa 1942.

The paratroops opposed themselves to this tactic, both remaining costantly in their fightning positions which were not protected during the preparatory fire, to be able to enter immediately in action on the enemy's arrival and opening fire all together at the minimum distance. Before doing this, however, they deliberately allowed the enemy to surpass them, to surprise him with the crossed fire of the automatic weapons on the flanks and rear. In this way, they managed to create disorder in the attackers who, though clearly superior as for men and weapons, found themselves in the terrible psychological condition of not feeling their back protected. Another apparently suicidal tactic, but in reality a largely winning, one was that of the 'preventive counterassault', adopted to avoid a direct engagement with bayonets that would have undoubtedly withnessed the enemy prevailing.

An Italian defensive position under attack.

Italian soldiers during an attack.

British *Crusader Mk III* tank during the Battle of El Alamein, Autumn 1942.

A *Folgore* paratrooper throws a grenade.

When the attackers where within a few dozen meters from the italian positions, the paratroopers leaped to counterattack throwing hand grenades just at the time when the enemy was more vulnerable. Taking advantage of the confusion created by their action their returned to their starting position. In this way, they cancelled the impact strenght of the attackers, disordered their ranks and reduced their morale. This explain how they succeeded even against forces ten times their number and without suffering large losses. The counterassault was emploîded against the tanks too using incendiary bottles and other contingency means that, if not able to stop the enemy totally, were equally able to overtake and slacken him (the British tankers too, seized with fear and confusion, suffered the negative psychological impact of these assaults). The winning engagement at Deir el Munassib on 30 September gained the *Folgore* the first citation on the Italian war bulletin. In such a circumstance the Division left its covering name and officially regained its original one. Thanks to its heroic behaviour in the battle, *Folgore* was very well know and feared by the enemy.

Sherman tanks of the Eighth Army move across the desert.

El Alamein

The final and decisive attack of the British against the sector defended by *Folgore* took place in the El Alamein battle in the days from 23 to 29 October 1942. Even many years after the end of the war our adversaires went on trying to minimize the strenght of this offensive, as if they wanted to reduce its real weight up to consider it a simple diversive manoeuvre. As a consequence all this would have artificially reduced the victory that *Folgore* won so brillantly in that situation. On the contrary, and this appear most of all from a deep study of the official British documents, the southern offensive was not a quiet secondary element in the attack plan as it aimed to unhinge all the Italo-German front with a turning manoeuvre from the southern sector.

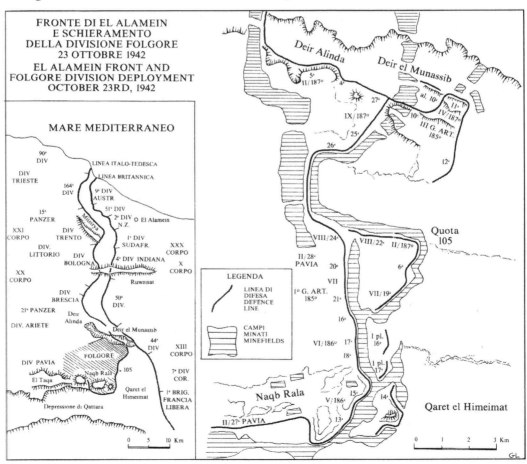

The Para Capt. Costantino Ruspoli di Poggio Suasa. Gold Metal to Military Valour, together with his brother Marescotti. Both fell as heroes during the El Alamein battle.

British Troops attack running past a knocked-out German Panzer MkIII tank, November 1942.

It was decided considering that the overpowering superiority of forces in that sector was an opportunity too valuable not to be immediately exploited with the maximum determination. And to be sure of the success, the British employed an attack force that would not have been at all justified by a simple diversive manoeuvre. The *Folgore* paratroops who were aware to constitute the last barrier before the rear area of the Italo-German Army, had prepared their defences along a front of about 15 kilometers, determined to sell dearly their skin. Instead of a single attack it was a series of offensives that gave way to four different fightings, the first one on 23 at 'quota 105' in the central sector, the second one in the North, near Naqb Rala on the 24, the third at 'quota 105' again on the 24 and 25, the last one in the South, on 25, 26 and 29 October, on the Munassib salient. To the repeated British attacks, the paratroops answered with incredibile determination and energy, throwing back every attempt to breach three lines and inflicting heavy losses to the enemy. Such an unespected resistance that lasted a week, forced the British commands to stop any further initiatives on that front. The El Alamein battle would be decided a few days later on the other fronts.

When on 2 November, following the order of general withdrawal, the *Folgore* left its positions its line of resistance was still intact. Once again the winning weapon of the paratroops was their net tactical superiority; the counterassault sistematically applied against the enemy's Tanks and infantry attacks cancelled their offensive powers. The training received at home aimed at developing and increasing besides the physical qualities also the morale and the courage, selfcontrol, initiative, had found in this situation its better application, considering moreover that it was these men's first true war experience. The *Folgore* paratroops had fully answered the trust placed on them, even if at high cost with about 1,100 losses in total dead, wounded and missing. The rest of the division would dissolve itself during the tragic withdrawal in the desert.

Folgore **paratroopers POW, November 1942.**

Folgore **paratroopers on the Takrouna stronghold.**

Tunisia

Captain Lombardini with the very few survivors that escaped death or prison succeded in reconstituting a battalion of about 600 men in the first days of December 1942 that was called 285th Folgore Parachute battalion. Attached to the 66th Infantry Regiment of the *Trieste* Division, the battalion had four companies plus an autonomous company attached to the 4th '*Granatieri di Sardegna*' battalion, that was also given as reinforcement to the 66th Infantry. To the unit was also added the Carabinieri parachute group of the disbanded 1st battalion. The *Folgore* battalion was engaged in the last fightings on Libyan ground and then, with the start of 1943, covered the withdrawal to Tunisia of the Italo-German Army, deploying at first along the Mareth fortified line then in the area of Uadi Akarit and, at last, at Enfidaville. Already engaged in hard fightings with the enemy during the months of March and April and reduced to 200 men only as a consequence of the serious losses, the battalion fought on 20 and 21 April 1943 at the Takrouna stronghold. An Assault patrol of paratroops succeeded in conquering the village, placed on a rocky hill, reaching it after climbing a steep uadi that was considered impraticable. They defended it up to the end of the following day when attacked by decisively superior enemy forces, resisting until the complete annihilation. With this last war action, the heroical actions of the *Folgore* on African ground pratically ended.

Bibliography
G.Lundari, "*I paracadutisti Italiani 1937/45*", Editrice Militare Italiana, Milano 1989

SS-Hauptsturmfuhrer Hans-Jörg Hartmann
III Batl. 'Nordland' regiment 5th SS division "Wiking

By Ken Niewiarowicz

This is a photo-essay based on a stack of Photo albums and documents from the estate of *SS-Hauptsturmführer* Hans-Jörg Hartmann, born in Berlin-Licterfeld on October 21, 1913. The associated text is drawn from the captions of the photos as well as information in the documents that are associated with this grouping.

Hitler youth photo; during the years before Hitler's 1933 take-over. Hartmann is at upper left.

As an SA member 1932.

Hartmann served nearly a year as a *Wachtmeister* with the *landespolizei* 1934-35.

Hartmann joined the SS on October 1, 1935; SS number 272.292. Above, after November 1936, with *SS standarte 'Germania'*.

in World War Two 1939-1945

Hartmann with *SS standarte 'Germania'*.

Hartmann at *SS-Junkerschule* of Bad Tölz.

The Hartmann Siblings. Sister Helga and Brother Milo, an officer with the *Luftwaffe*.

With the *Verfügungstruppe* 1937. Note *'Germania'* cuff titles.

Hartmann takes aim with a Dreyse model 1907 automatic pistol, made by Rheinmetal. The Ugliest German pistol ever made.

Soldiers of *SS-Standarte 'Germania'* during a training march.

Junkerschule Tolz: April 1, 1938. Hartmann entered the *SS-Junkerschule* at Bad Tölz as a *StandartenJunker* (officer candidate).

Left: the Imposing main gate of Junkershule Tölz. Right: Hartmann (on the left) with a comrade in the picturesque alpen region of southern Bavaria.

Hartmann with two friends. Note the Cuff title on the overcoat sleeve at right. *"SS Schule Tölz"*.

A field exercise with senior officers at Bad Tölz.

Newly minted officers from the Junkerschule Bad Tölz.

Hartmann appears at center foreground second from the left of the rank.

in World War Two 1939-1945

According to a personal review by the commander of the Junkerschule Tolz in July of 1938: "*Hartmann has a solid, impeccable character. Physically mediocre, his services are sufficient and better. In recent times, he has suffered from bad family circumstances; this is also due to the lack of concentration. Lack of front service and short training time still allow him sufficient achievements in practical service. His level of performance at the front is still uncertain. Guidance in and out of service was very good. In relations, especially with superiors, he is calm and reserved, yet trusting. Hartmann is still capable of development in his life and will become a useful leader with the appropriate performance*".

October 1-10 1938. After the Munich accord, German troops move to occupy the Sudetenland.

SS-Standarte 'Germania' took part in the occupation, integrated with army units. Here, German soldiers crossing the former border. Apparently Hartmann recognized the historical significance of taking this photograph at this particular place.

'Germania' troops entering predominantly German towns are welcomed enthusiastically by the inhabitants. Note the rifles carried are WW1 vintage G98s used widely by SS-VT units.

The Czech army was ordered not to resist. These two Czech soldiers must appear as a curiosity to the advancing soldiers of *'Germania'*.

According to a performance overview by the commander of the "Germania" replacement battalion in February 1940, Hartmann is of moderate physical size. (Hartman was 5'8") his official appearance leaves something to be desired. This small lack of appearance does not allow for personal performance. Hartmann has a tendency to softness as a superior, which has a detrimental effect on the education of underlings and men (especially in times of war). [However] through the influence of his company commander and his work on himself, he has acquired the respect and trust of his subordinates. He was involved in the Polish campaign as MG platoon leader and was wounded [in the upper right arm]. At his request and the existing inclination he was transferred to the [75mm] infantry gun replacement company. Hartmann was promoted to *SS-Obersturmführer* on August 1, 1940; attached to 4th company, SS regiment *'Nordland'* as part of the cadre of German officers around which was built the predominantly Dutch, Danish, Scandinavian unit later attached to 5th SS Panzer division *'Wiking'*. In April of 1941, Hartmann was given command of 12th company regiment *'Nordland'* prior to moving in position for the attack on Russia in June.

(To be continued)

in World War Two 1939-1945

Slovakian army in WW2
By Rene Chavez

Map of Slovakia, 1939.

Slovak Minister of National Defense General Ferdinand Čatloš awarding ethnic Germans serving in the Slovak Army after the Polish campaign.

Hitler and Monsignor Jozef Tiso at Berlin, 1939.

Because of the fear of having a war with Germany, an International conference was held by France and Great Britain where a decision was made to allow Germany the right to annex the borderline region composed of 50% of "volksdeutsche" (ethnic Germans). In 1938, Germany in a bloodless takeover invaded the western part of Czechoslovakia. First claiming the borderline region known as the "Sudetenland" where three million ethnic-Germans lived. The western part of Czechoslovakia after the government abdicated was named by the Germans as the protectorate state of Bohemia-Moravia. The eastern part of Czechoslovakia was the separatist country of Slovakia, which has always desired autonomy from their Czech neighbors. In March 1939, with German military support the Slovakian Puppet State was formed. Slovakia was governed under Premier Monsignor Jozef Tiso who set up his own para-military militia called the "*Hlinka Guards*", modeled on Germany's SA Storm Troopers. Slovakia had its own military composed of former members of the Czechoslovakian Army, which included Volksdeutsche personnel. Eager to prove its willingness to serve on the German side, Slovakia formed two combat mobile groups, organized around the 1st and 3rd Slovak Infantry Divisions. In September 1939, these mobile groups were used during the German invasion of Poland, claiming territory that was theirs. By June 1941, Slovakia was one of the first foreign countries to provide military support in Operation *Barbarossa* in what the Germans called the crusade against Bolshevism. The Slovakian Army Corps, which had the 1st and 2nd Infantry Divisions, crossed into the Soviet Union and began operations in southern Russia.

A *LT-35* light tank of the Slovak Army in western Ukraine.

Slovak motorized infantry.

About 42,000 Slovakians were sent to the Eastern Front. Almost immediately the Slovakian Army Corps fell behind the German mobile forces crossing the vast Russian landscape. As a result a fast mobile brigade was formed, capable of keeping fast pace with the Germans. This independent brigade was placed permanently under German 17th Army Command, which was part of Army Group South.

Soldiers of the Slovak Mobile Division on the Eastern Front.

Slovakian Schnelle Division

By August 1941, the rest of the corps was brought home for refitting. The Slovaks created two new divisions, a 10,000 strong mechanized "*Slowakische Schnelle Division*" (Slovakian Swift Division) and a security division of 6000 men. The Schnelle Division was formed from personnel of the 1st Infantry Division and from members of the brigade and was under the command of Gustav Malar. In September 1941, the Schnelle Division was placed under German command and sent to the Ukrainian front near Kiev. The Schnelle Division, which the majority was of German Volkdeustche personnel, was in the Mius River where it fought hard against the Russians during the winter of 1941-42. In late 1942, the 31st Artillery Regiment of the Slovakian Security Division was transferred to the Schnelle Division. In

January 1943, the command of the division was changed and assigned to Lt. Gen. Jurech. The division along side the German SS *Wiking* Division took part in the capture of Rostov, there it advanced into the Kuban region with the 1st German Panzer Army.

Members of Slovak Fast division crossing river Dnepr, 1942.

Slovakian soldiers.

A Slovak *LT-40* light tank in Caucasus.

It helped to cover the retreat of German troops from the Caucasus Region after Stalingrad, and was nearly cut-off near Krasnodar. They were airlifted to the Crimean region, leaving their heavy equipment behind. Command of the division once again changed and placed under Lt. Gen. Elmir Lendvay. The Schnelle Division was sent to the front lines near the region of Melitopol, where the division was caught by a massive Russian formation that broke through the German lines. While surrounded, 2000 men of the division deserted to the Russian side. After a constant defensive struggle, the remnants of the division managed to escape. On 2 August 1943, the remnants of the division was pulled out and refitted to form a new unit. By 1943, the division was re-organized as the *1.Slowakische Infanterie Division* and was used for

Slovak defensive positions in Crimea, 1943.

coastal duties near the Crimean region. Morale with the troops began to deteriorate and men were lost due to desertions. Meanwhile a Security division was used for rear actions against partisans. The security division remained serving at the Ukrainian front.

Slovak pioneers on the eastern front.

Slovak cavalrymen.

Slovakian government suggested sending troops to the Balkans or Western Europe, but were turn down by the Germans. They then asked withdrawing to Slovakia, but the Germans again refused. When a Russian offensive broke through their coastal lines the Slovakians became unreliable and barely held on to their defensive positions.

In 1944, they were pulled out from the front and sent back to Slovakia were they were disarmed and converted into construction brigades. Meanwhile two new divisions were formed and used for defensive purposes in the Carpathians. A third division was being formed in central Slovakia when a Partisan uprising movement initiated in August 1944. However the Germans were able to disarmed the field divisions. Many of the soldiers deserted their post and joined the partisans who were being helped by an allied Czechoslovakian Airborne Brigade flown in by the Russians. In

in World War Two 1939-1945

February 1945, the puppet government of Tiso amounted to only one loyal infantry regiment composed of Hlinka Guards, a flak regiment and an artillery battery.

Slovakia Schnelle Division Badge

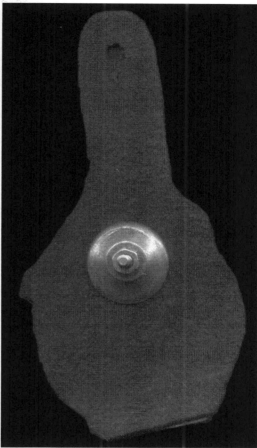

The badge design shows a wreath of laurel leaves with an eagle on top. The eagle is clutching in its talons the initials "R D" indicating *"Rychlé divise"* (Rapid Division). Below the initials you can clearly see a motorized tractor illustrating the truck radiator with the year (1941, 42-43) posted in the center. The badge has also been found with years 1941-1942. The reverse is solid and flat. The original production for the badge was crudely made by the division automotive workshops and they were cast. The material used for the production of the badges was mostly composed of metal bearings such as zinc. The size varies a little mostly 54mm x 47mm. The badges were attached to the uniform with a screw and nut. Some badges are polished, chrome, some are certainly nicer than others, but all are interesting example of the campaign against the Soviet Union. The Slovakians made another award modeled to the German Army (Crimean shield). This badge was also made in the automotive workshops. The badge is also crudely made and is similar to the Rapid badge, the difference is that it has the Crimean peninsula and the year 1943-44 inscribed below the thin wreath. The size is 51 mm.

Slovakian Eastern Front Award

Shown below is the bronze and silver class Slovakian Eastern Front awards. The Badge of Honor for service in the Eastern Front.

Slovak soldiers taking cover in a rye field near Lypovets in Ukraine.

The Slovakians who participated on the Eastern Front were awarded with a bronze, silver or combined bronze and silver campaign badge. The badge was instituted on 22 April 1942 and produced by the Slovak Mint in Kremnica. The bronze badge pictured above shows a Slovakian Helmet with the date inscribed "22 VI 1941" indicating the date the Slovakian Army participated in the Eastern Front. On the background is a sword crushing the communist symbolic star and the hammer and sickle. The reverse is solid and concave shape. It contains a small pin and catch. The criteria for these awards were the following classes:

- The silver class was awarded for combatants.
- The bronze and silver was awarded for support units. This badge has a silver wreath and sword with the remainder in bronze.
- The bronze for rear echelon personnel.

WW2 AXIS
FORCES

Made in the USA
Middletown, DE
17 February 2020

84912758R00044